Intermediate
Literacy Stations

Intermediate
Literacy Stations

Susan Nations and Sandy Waite

Maupin House

Intermediate Literacy Stations

© 2009 Susan Nations and Sandy Waite. All Rights Reserved.

Cover design: Studio Montage
Book design and layout: Mickey Cuthbertson

Library of Congress Cataloging-in-Publication Data

Nations, Susan.
  Intermediate literacy stations / Susan Nations and Sandy Waite.
      p. cm.
  Includes bibliographical references.
  ISBN 978-1-934338-42-1 (pbk.)
  1. Language arts (Middle school)--Activity programs. I. Waite, Sandy, 1961- II. Title.
  LB1631.N32 2009
  428.0071'2--dc22
                                    2009011306

Maupin House publishes professional resources for K-12 educators. Contact us for tailored, in-school training or to schedule an author for a workshop or conference. Visit www.maupinhouse.com for free lesson plan downloads.

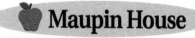
Maupin House

Maupin House Publishing, Inc.
2416 NW 71 Place
Gainesville, FL 32653
www.maupinhouse.com
800-524-0634
352-373-5588
352-373-5546 (fax)
info@maupinhouse.com
10 9 8 7 6 5 4 3 2 1

Acknowledgments

Again and again when we are in the midst of our colleagues we hear the question,"When are you going to put your ideas in a book?"Workshop by workshop, lesson by lesson, and collaboration by collaboration, *Intermediate Literacy Stations* was born. It is a true convergence of our own thinking, learning, and research, along with teacher inquiry and input. It is filled with classroom-tested and student-approved activities.

It would be impossible to name each teacher and student by name that has had a hand in the creation of this book and/or the activities in it. We are, however, grateful for your expertise and willingness to help us get it right. It has been a fun process that prodded our thinking and helped us grow.

Steve Dragon, our principal, and Mary Rozelle, our assistant principal, continually promote literacy and learning on our school's campus. No organization moves in a positive direction without excellent leaders at the top. It is our privilege to work under top quality leadership each and every day.

The amazing faculty and staff at Gocio Elementary School continue to provide meaningful literacy experiences for our students. It is a joy to work with so many talented people! Your input on many of these activities is invaluable!

To the kids in Sandy's class this year who have tested each of these stations and allowed us to photograph them (again and again and again): Aaron, Alexis, Austin, Bryanna, De'Arron, Devin, Gaspar, Isaiah, Jasiah, Karrington, Kayla, Kenya, Kiyara, Larry, Luisa, Miranda, Rebecca, Tyler, and Van. We are so proud of you and the literacy learners you are!

Suzi Boyett, Kristin Boerger, and Debra Voege, our friends and colleagues, have spent countless hours visiting and revisiting the stations in this book via phone, email, and even on long car trips. Their conversation and questions are what help us continually refine each activity to make it better for kids.

From Susan

When a new book is on the verge of being published, I find myself quite reflective. I know that there are so many people who make it possible. Some who know and some who don't.

As always, I have to thank my husband, Don, my soulmate, for his love and friendship for so many years. Your steadfast love and belief in me and my calling to work in education is as natural as breathing is for you. I love you and am grateful for each gentle nudge to continue writing and complete another project!

My children continue to teach and inspire me in ways they may never understand. From Daniel, I have learned determination and drive to finish what is started while not being afraid to shift gears when necessary. Matthew reminds me to seek passion and pursue excellence all the while never losing sight of who I am or where I've been. Jordan exudes perseverance, focus, and the importance of learning all you can about your interests and life's work. Aaron is a constant reminder to find joy in the little things and always keep a song in your heart. You are each a constant blessing to me! I love you!

From Sandy

Writing this book has been a very special time for me. While Susan has gone through this process numerous times before, this is my first book. It has been an incredible journey filled with learning, laughter, and patience. My passion for teaching literacy has grown deeper than I could ever have imagined. I need to thank Susan for her friendship and for helping me grow in this process.

I want to thank my husband, Steve, for always being the best friend I could ever have. I know I can count on you for honest opinions, understanding, and encouragement. Thank you for sharing this exciting new venture with me and supporting me every step of the way. I love you and all you are.

My daughters have been two of the best things in my life. Lindsey, your creativity in your music, your cooking, and everything you try is limitless. Your dedication to what you believe in is admirable. Megan, your determination and desire to forge ahead, even when obstacles are in the road, show your true character. Your gentleness and kindness to all always warms my heart. You have both grown into beautiful young women and are an inspiration to me.

Table of Contents

Chapter 4: Planning and Establishing the Literacy Learning Cycle 31

Chapter 5: More Ideas for Station Management and Planning 37

Part Two: The Stations, Strategies, And Activities 47

Chapter 6: Comprehension 49

Pages	Activity Name	Strategy Focus
50-53	Author's Study	Compare and contrast
54-57	Let's Take a Trip	Monitoring understanding; Finding details to respond to questions in informational text
58-60	Search and Summarize	Locating teacher-designated Target Skill® in fiction or non-fiction text; Writing concise summaries
61-64	Senses Brainstorm	Making connections using schema; Relating to characters in text
65-68	True/False Trivia	Finding relevant and useful information; Using details to determine fact vs. opinion

Chapter 10: Word Work 141

Pages	Activity Name	Strategy Focus
142-143	Grab a Word, Make a Sentence	Use new vocabulary that is directly taught
144-145	Making Words	Creating words; Using dictionaries to confirm the meaning of new vocabulary words
146-149	Poetry Place	Identify and explain how language choice helps to develop mood and meaning in poetry; Use context clues to determine meaning of unknown words
150-155	Prefix/Suffix Word Play	Use meaning of familiar base word and affixes to create and determine the meaning of new words
156-158	Word Gathering	Categorize key vocabulary

Chapter 11: Written Response 159

Pages	Activity Name	Strategy Focus
160-164	Create-a-Story Matrix	Identify characters, setting, and problem; Brainstorm ideas; Narrative writing
165-168	Digging Deeper	Informational text research and written response; Compare text for further details
169-176	My Reading Journal	Write in various formats; Respond to specific questions based on fiction or non-fiction text
177-180	Nose for News	News article writing; Respond to specific headlines and topic questions
181-183	What a Character!	Character trait descriptions based on reading; Give support and evidence in writing

Downloadable Color Reproducibles

Reproducible	Page
Author's Study cover	51
Author's Study student directions	52
Let's Take a Trip cover	55
Let's Take a Trip student directions	56
Search and Summarize cover	59
Senses Brainstorm cover	62
Senses Brainstorm student directions	63
True/False Trivia cover	66
True/False Trivia student directions	67
Found Poem cover	71
Little Buddy cover	76
Little Buddy student directions	77
One-Minute Reading cover	80
One-Minute Reading student directions	81
Reader's Theater cover	85
Recording Studio cover	88
Recording Studio student directions	89
Computer Presentation student directions	93
Computer Presentation fiction sample	94
Computer Presentation informational text sample	95
Karaoke cover	97
Merry-Go-Round Reading student directions	100
Question Me answer flap	102
Question Me question cards	105-112
Research and Present It presentation ideas sheet	118
Create a Model cover	123
Create a Model student directions	124
Create a Scene cover	128
Create a Scene student directions	129
Food for Thought cover	132
Food for Thought student directions	133
Vocabulary Chains cover	135
Vocabulary Chains student directions	136
Vocabulary Word Art cover	139
Vocabulary Word Art student directions	140
Grab a Word, Make a Sentence student directions	143
Making Words student directions	145
Poetry Place forms	147-149
Prefix/Suffix Word Play student directions	151
Word Gathering student directions	157
Create-a-Story Matrix cover	162
Create-a-Story Matrix student directions	163
Digging Deeper cover	166
Digging Deeper student directions	167
My Reading Journal student directions	170
My Reading Journal cover	171
My Reading Journal cards	173-176
Nose for News student directions	178
What a Character title page	182

Introduction

A wide range of texts and literacy materials is found throughout the intermediate reading classroom. Students are joyfully working independently, in small groups, and with the teacher. All students are engaged and on task and seem to know exactly what the routines and procedures are without constant direction. The room and the activities within it appear to run like a well-oiled machine. No space remains unused for learning and inquiry.

This is just a glimpse of an engaging literacy environment. It should be the goal of every teacher of reading to create such a place where learning is deep and meaningful for all students, regardless of age or reading level.

As we conduct workshops for educators, again and again we hear teachers of older students asking for help in creating such a space. They want to provide their students with meaningful literacy tasks so that they can differentiate and teach small groups. But teachers are overwhelmed. And they don't want stations that look "too babyish." When intermediate teachers look at their primary counterparts, they often see twelve to fifteen active centers in the same classroom. They wonder just how they can manage that much while also teaching the content areas and test-taking strategies that so often fill the day.

Intermediate teachers also face the dilemma of higher curriculum expectations in the classroom. This means that they must integrate more and teach with more depth and complexity. For these reasons, we believe the intermediate classroom is more sophisticated. Since the work that is happening with older students is more sophisticated, we decided to use a more sophisticated term for the work that happens during small-group instruction. Rather than "centers," we call them stations. Students like the term and feel it separates them from the primary students in the school.

When we ourselves started using literacy stations with intermediate students, we found that less is sometimes more. It is easy to believe that older children can and should handle MORE activities during their workshop than younger students. More is not always better, however; depth and complexity should be the goals. Completing a few activities over an extended time encourages less unnecessary movement in the classroom and more time to investigate literacy acquisition. More time investigating text creates further opportunities for deep reading and critical thinking.

It comes down to helping students become literacy investigators. They are thinking about text critically, asking questions, and drawing conclusions based on their interactions. If investigation is the core of how we want students working with text, then each and every station must lead to investigation, and literacy activities within each station must be selected and created wisely.

What You Will Find in This Book

This book is divided into two parts. **Part One** provides you with all the basics and classroom-tested tips for establishing and maintaining stations in your classroom.

- **Chapter 1:** Follow the reader's workshop model to help students move toward independence as they practice and apply literacy skills in six intermediate stations: Comprehension, Fluency, Listening and Speaking, Visual Literacy, Word Work, and Written Response.

- **Chapter 2:** Choose and differentiate activities that encourage the deepest level of investigation from your students.

- **Chapter 3:** Learn how to keep students moving from station to station as they take control of their own learning by using a Literacy Learning Plan that outlines their station rotations.

- **Chapter 4:** Start your stations and manage activities with a station rotation table.

- **Chapter 5:** Use insider tips and tricks for planning lessons, keeping activities fresh and students on track and organized.

Part Two has six chapters, each focusing on a suggested literacy station and offering five activities, complete with material lists, tips for setting up, step-by-step activity instructions, strategies for differentiation, and reproducibles. Full-color reproducibles of the literacy station activity titles, student directions, and other pages are available for download at www.maupinhouse.com/pdf/IntermediateLiteracyStations.zip.

Look for this icon on the pages throughout the book that are available in color.

PART ONE

Independent Investigation
With Literacy Stations

Chapter 1
The Literacy Station Framework

Stations and Activities

Let's establish a shared definition of intermediate literacy stations to use throughout this book.

A **station** is a place in the classroom designed to help students practice and apply literacy skills and strategies.

Stations are focused on the key components of reading instruction: comprehension, fluency, oral language, phonics, phonemic awareness, and vocabulary. For our purposes, we have combined the final three areas (phonics, phonemic awareness, and vocabulary) into word work. We recognize, however, that other areas of literacy development can be ignored when we only focus on these six. After careful review of the NCTE/IRA literacy standards, we created our stations for the intermediate classroom. The stations we suggest are Comprehension, Fluency, Listening and Speaking, Visual Literacy, Word Work, and Written Response. These encompass all the components of reading instruction and more and are explained in detail at the end of this chapter.

While a station could be a designated physical space in the classroom, it may also simply be a tub of materials or an envelope that will be needed to complete an activity. Whether you choose to create specific spaces for students to visit and complete activities or simply a space to hold materials needed to complete activities on the floor or in a seat, make sure each station is consistent. This way, students can focus on the most meaningful tasks during station time: literacy acquisition.

A **station activity** is a task within the station that reinforces a particular skill or strategy.

Teachers continually tell us they do not have "time to teach." It is, therefore, most important that each and every activity completed in the classroom during station time be meaningful to students. Following is the list of criteria we use to determine if an activity will be meaningful in the context of an intermediate literacy classroom and lead students to authentic literacy investigations:

Station activities should

- Invite students to practice and apply the skills and strategies that were previously taught and modeled;

- Promote reading, writing, speaking, listening, and viewing;

- Investigate text in a variety of genres;

- Build and extend vocabulary;

- Practice and develop fluency;

- Enrich learning and comprehension across the content areas;

- Be open-ended and engaging; and

- Enable teacher assessment and evaluation of students' application of literacy skills and strategies.

Literacy stations and the activities that take place within them are only one piece of the classroom literacy puzzle. In fact, to create truly meaningful experiences, an instructional framework must be in place. We have built our classrooms around the Gradual Release of Responsibility Model.

Gradual Release of Responsibility

Think about how you learn. It doesn't matter whether you are learning to cook, fly, dive, or even teach differently. A common framework is always in place to guide learning. We generally seek out and observe a model first. Then we find someone who will mentor us as we practice the new skill together. Gradually, the mentor will become a coach as we practice our new learning. Finally, we must have time to try our new skill in our own setting or context.

In education, P. David Pearson calls this model the Gradual Release of Responsibility (1983). As teachers, we are the models who monitor and decide when students are ready to shift roles with us as they implement their new learning. The goal is for less and less support from us and more and more independence for students.

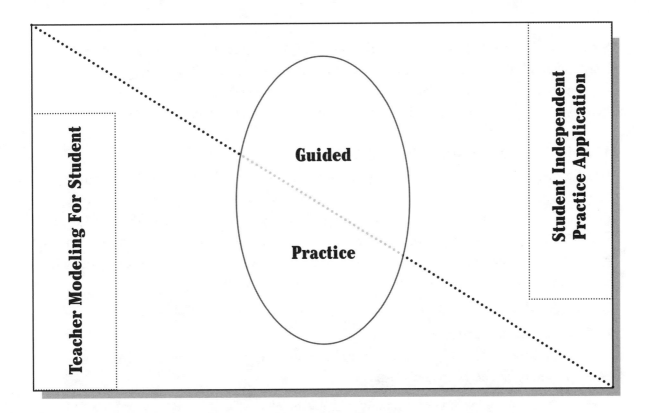

This graphic is based on work by Pearson and Gallagher (1983). In a later study, Fielding and Pearson (1994) identified four components of instruction that follow the path of the Gradual Release of Responsibility Model: teacher modeling, guided practice, independent practice, and application. Application occurs when students can take what they have practiced and apply it in a new situation or context.

When students enter third grade and beyond, we often assume they are ready to apply directly after the teacher models. Think of all the lectures you have heard. It's like the person is up there, presenting information with a great deal of confidence that you will put their content directly into practice. This is not always the case. There are times that even the adult learner needs to practice with the model and alone in order to hone a new skill.

We must be careful not to take away the all-important shared and guided learning time and meaningful practice time. We must create classrooms where students are free to move back and forth along the learning continuum throughout the day. Our job is to know when they need more support, or scaffolding, from us and gradually when to remove that support.

The Reader's Workshop Model

A **workshop** is a structured time where students can interact with texts, the teacher, and their peers through meaningful literacy experiences.

Simply to surround students with quality books and expect them to "get it" is not enough. Teaching and learning must be explicit and systematic. The literacy continuum must be experienced again and again through the reader's workshop model, where there is a true give and take between modeling, guiding, and student practice and application of the learning.

Modeled Reading: Reading *to* Students

Read-aloud: The read-aloud is your opportunity to model for students the kinds of thinking they should be doing when they read their own books. These shared experiences are perfect opportunities to set the tone for the workshop and allow you to "act as the author and the reader" (Mooney, 1990). When you read, you are giving students a glimpse into the thinking that goes on in the mind of a good reader. This is a time to allow students to discuss key ideas with you, answer a focus question, or make a connection to their writing.

> ### *Think About It: Read-Aloud*
> - Use a variety of genres and texts. Include current events, content materials, poetry, picture books, and chapter books.
> - Make the material you select readily available to your students so they can revisit and dig deeper into familiar text.
> - Consider reading only a snippet (one or two chapters) of a chapter book, and then make it available for independent readers to finish later.
> - Model your thinking using stems like: *I notice..., I wonder..., I think...,* and *I learned...*

Shared Reading: Reading *with* Students

Shared reading: With shared reading, students have visual access to the text, and you explicitly and systematically teach and demonstrate essential reading skills and strategies identified by your district and/or state curriculum. Shared reading materials will primarily be whatever the core reading material is in your school or district. With the increasing availability of digital equipment in schools, the possibilities for shared reading are expanded greatly. Teachers can enlarge almost any text and make it interactive using an interactive whiteboard or other digital medium. The pacing for shared-reading instruction should be lively and demonstrate teacher engagement. This, in turn, leads to student involvement in the lesson.

Think About It: Shared Reading

- Use your core reading materials to guide your instruction.

- Supplement and enrich core reading materials with other books and resource materials—such as trade books, Big Books, posters, charts, magazines, and newspaper articles—to practice the weekly focus skill or strategy.

- Focus on one or two core reading objectives and weave them throughout your reading block. For example, have students practice a key comprehension strategy in their small group after you complete the whole-class lesson.

- Set some time aside to teach and model test-taking strategies.

Differentiation: Reading *by* Students with Teacher Support

Small-group instruction: This instruction is generally delivered to a group of six to eight students with an applied literacy focus as you revisit a previous whole-class lesson or pre-teach a focus skill lesson planned for later. By using a text that students can read with 90–94 percent accuracy, their focus is on deciphering meaning and practicing a skill or concept from the whole-group lesson. Groups are differentiated based on students' current learning needs. Remember that grouping by need may not always mean grouping students at similar levels; you may also group in order to teach and model thinking or other good reading behaviors.

Think About It: Differentiation

- Groups should be flexible and based on students' current literacy needs.

- Materials will vary based on student needs and can include leveled guided-reading books, classroom library books, articles, and magazines.

- Lessons will be at the word, text, or meaning level.

- Once you set the tone and focus for the group, you are more of a coach during this time.

- Use ongoing observational data and progress monitoring to identify common needs and plan your small-group instruction.

Independent Reading: Reading *by* Students Alone

Independent reading and literacy stations: Students navigate through text experiences and activities both independently and with their peers as they practice and apply what has been taught and modeled in shared and guided experiences. Students self-select anchor texts—texts used to complete each station activity during a two-week cycle—that they will read and respond to during this time (see pp. 26-27). Their selection may be based on interest or book level.

In his book, *Around the Reading Workshop in 180 Days* (Heinemann, 2006), author Frank Serafini notes: "The reading workshop is nothing more than an organizational framework for reading instruction. That's it! It is not a program to be delivered, nor is it a series of scripted lessons. It is a structure within which to locate reading instruction that provides an array of learning experiences for developing proficient, sophisticated readers" (p. 21).

When we set our classrooms up with such a structure, we are setting students up for success and engagement in their own literacy acquisition. In order to implement a reader's workshop model effectively, the classroom must be filled with a variety of texts with which students can practice and apply their literacy skills and strategies.

Engagement Starts with Text

The Classroom Library

No matter what literacy research you read or what grade level you teach, there is one commonly held belief: the literate classroom cannot exist unless it houses a well-stocked classroom library. The classroom library is the foundation for all of the stations in this book. It is the place where text options are housed and where students choose, negotiate, and apply literacy learning to text that interests them. It is the core of the classroom.

The classroom library, according to Regie Routman in her book, *Reading Essentials* (2003), should be the "hub" of the classroom. And, in her later book, *Teaching Essentials* (2008), Routman notes that schools and districts should "put money and efforts into developing magnificent school and classroom libraries. Access to books and a wide variety of excellent reading materials and genres have the potential to do more to increase achievement than any advanced technology."

Here are some things to consider whether you have a classroom library that just needs sprucing up or are starting from scratch.

- **Set a goal of starting with ten books per student in your classroom.** You will want to add to your collection gradually so that you have a wide range of genres and book levels from which students can select anchor texts. Many teachers build their library by seeking book donations from parents, applying for grants, using book club points, or hitting garage sales and used bookstores.

- **The library should be well-organized and visually attractive to readers.** Think about the appeal of bookstore cafés: comfortable seating; books displayed with covers facing out; a wide range of levels and genres available; well-lit. Set your library up with the same focus. Include some comfortable chairs or a rug. Display some covers facing out to make book selection easier. Include picture books as well as chapter books. Store books in baskets or bins according to author, genre, theme or topic, and occasionally readability (although we try to use this very little if at all). If possible, include some lamps for homier lighting.

- **Include your students in setting up.** If students help create the baskets and sort books, they will have a better understanding of the anchor texts available to them for each cycle. If possible, allow them to make donations to the library as well.

From Susan: When I taught a group of third-grade students at a Title I school, I found they weren't able to bring books in for our library. I still wanted students' input on the books for their library, however. I used some of my book club points and allowed each child to shop with the points in the book club catalog. When the books arrived, we created a book plate that said, "This book especially selected for Mrs. Nations' library by [insert child's name]." The students absolutely loved knowing they had personally contributed to the books in our classroom. And they really loved it when they moved on and realized they were leaving something behind for future students.

At the core of each literacy station and its activities is the anchor text that students self-select and use to complete their contracted work over the two-week work cycle (further explained in chapter 3). It's important that you are continually adding new books in order to keep the anchor text selection fresh and engaging for students.

Use the following checklist to assess your classroom library.

Does your classroom library...	YES	NO
Have at least 8–10 quality titles per student in your classroom?		
Have tubs or baskets to house similar books by author, genre, or topic?		
Give students easy access to books with titles facing outward and un-crowded shelves for easy browsing?		
Have books representing multiple levels and interests to appeal to your students?		
Allow students to check out books and take them home?		
Include books that students have helped select?		
Have current books that interest students?		
Include comfortable places to sit and browse through books?		
Include multiple copies of popular titles to encourage group discussions?		
Contain a variety of text (books, magazines, graphic novels, newspapers, etc.)		

Preparing Space for Stations

When considering stations for your classroom, it is important to think about and envision what your classroom will look like. We find that keeping six stations with some additional options for free choice works best. Students are asked to create their work plan in a two-week literacy cycle in order to give them time to delve deeply into text and respond with insight and inquiry. The classroom should be set up in such a way that students have ample access to a variety of texts.

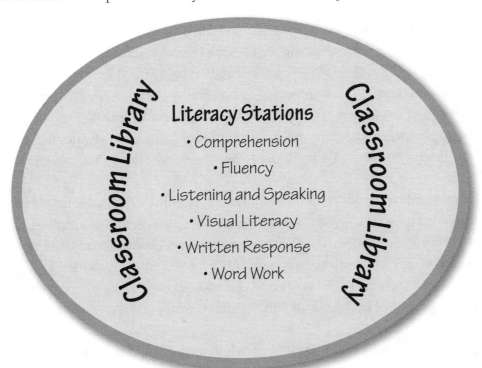

Classroom Library

Literacy Stations
- Comprehension
- Fluency
- Listening and Speaking
- Visual Literacy
- Written Response
- Word Work

Classroom Library

Remember that each station activity works in concert with the classroom library to make a meaningful station time. Within each station there will be one to two activities for students to practice and apply their use of skills and strategies during the two-week literacy cycle.

Stations to Include

The six stations we suggest using in all intermediate classrooms, and upon which this book is built, are Comprehension, Fluency, Listening and Speaking, Visual Literacy, Word Work, and Written Response.

Remember that stations are the places that house the activity choices for the literacy cycle. You could complete a set-up in such a way that students go TO a station. You can also set up stations so that students can access materials and take them to their own space in the classroom. Whatever set up you choose, make sure your students know and understand the purpose for each station and how to access the text to complete each station activity they select.

Comprehension. Why do you read? The real purpose of reading is so that you can make connections between what you read—the text—and what you already know—your schema. We want our students truly to understand the text, to perceive and really investigate the ideas about which they read. Reading isn't just something that happens when you say the words; you really need to think about it. There are seven key comprehension strategies that foster the ties between reading and thinking: using schema, predicting/inferring, monitoring, questioning, determining importance, visualizing, and synthesizing/summarizing. Activities in this station help students practice using the key strategies to become better readers and thinkers.

Fluency. Fluent reading sounds natural and flowing and has meaning that is unbroken. Because fluent readers don't have to worry about decoding words, their attention can be directed to the meaning of what they are reading. They read with prosody and make appropriate inflections based on the meaning of the text. Students who are fluent readers also will have a stronger self-image and more confidence for public speaking. Activities at the fluency station offer a range of opportunities to practice reading orally with a partner, independently, and in a small group.

Listening and Speaking. A listening skill is different from a "hearing" ability. While students may hear what you are saying, or hear one another, how well do they really listen? When we talk about listening, we are referring to an active, attentive listening. Students need to know that listeners keep their eyes on the speaker, listen respectfully, and if appropriate for the situation, respond to what the speaker is saying. Speakers, likewise, need to do more than just talk. Students need to pace their words—not too slow, not too fast; and they need to pronounce clearly what they read. Knowing what type of voice to use in any given situation is important.

Visual Literacy. Visual literacy is what we can see and perceive visually. Visual texts are those that convey their meanings through images, various patterns, charts, and diagrams. There may be words included, but this isn't always the case. Visual texts are sometimes hard copies of texts and other times they are electronic. Students who are able to represent their thinking and learning through art and creative expression are practicing their visual literacy.

Written Response. Not only do students need to be able to express their thinking about texts in formal and informal conversations, they also need to be able to write about what they have read. Very often, intermediate students are required to write about their reading for state-wide tests and/or classroom assessments. Students need to communicate clearly about the text they read whether it is fictional or informational. Written response provides them another venue to demonstrate their understanding of the text.

Word Work. Word work encompasses working with words in a variety of ways. Students should become familiar with vocabulary in the text they are using. They should be able to think critically about the meanings of words and connect them through categorizing. Students should use word meanings and origins to figure out other words. They also should know how words and letters work to help them learn unfamiliar words.

Creating Activities for Stations

Part Two of this book is divided into six chapters, one for each of the literacy stations described previously. In each chapter, you will find five activities to use in that station. The activities work for many different genres and levels of texts. Each activity page includes directions for preparing the activity and introducing it to students and notes for differentiation for various levels of students.

Construct the activities that you will be using according to the teacher instruction pages. Follow the guidelines for introducing each activity to your students. Model each step of the directions. For step-by-step lessons on introducing the concept of a Literacy Cycle, see pages 31-33.

Make activities multidimensional to cover more skills and strategies. Consider the Search and Summarize station (p. 58), for example. It can be used for just about any Target Skill® you want students to search for in the text, plus it gives them practice writing summaries. Create it once, and you use it again and again! Time is too precious to make only one-dimensional activities.

Chapter 2
Discovering the Why—Digging Deeper in Stations

Consider the Why

From Susan: One of my first jobs as a new teacher was teaching third grade. This was back when file folder games and simple activity centers were all the rage. I spent hours creating materials for my third graders, oblivious to whether the skill was even something my kids needed! In fact, I actually remember choosing activities because they were "cute" and I thought my kids would "love them."

Certainly teachers are more focused on curriculum expectations today than they were twenty years ago. But some teachers still teach without really considering the *why* of their instruction. It is easy to respond to this simple question with "Because I need something to keep my kids busy so I can teach" or "Because my administrator says I have to implement literacy stations." Neither answer is wrong, but the true answer to "Why?" needs to be deeper than that. Much deeper.

Let's consider again the criteria we presented for literacy stations in the opening pages. A literacy station must

- Invite students to practice and apply the skills and strategies that were previously taught and modeled;
- Promote reading, writing, speaking, listening, and viewing;
- Investigate text in a variety of genres;
- Build and extend vocabulary;
- Practice and develop fluency;
- Enrich learning and comprehension across the content areas;
- Be open-ended and engaging; and
- Enable teacher assessment and evaluation of students' application of literacy skills and strategies.

Professional educators know that these indicators answer the question "Why do literacy stations at all?"

Invite Practice and Application of Skills and Strategies You Have Taught

Acquiring any new knowledge requires practice. We seem to lose sight of this as we age. Think about it. We allow young children to make approximations with almost everything they do. When they learn to walk, they are clumsy. When they learn to talk, their subjects and verbs don't match. All we do is praise the effort while modeling the correct implementation.

Early childhood teachers get it. They often have exploratory learning activities in the classroom. Some intermediate teachers get it. However, as students get older, the less often educators allow such approximations. We find many omit the safe practice in the interest of "time" and grades. Yet, many visual and performing artists will tell us that what they do is about eighty percent practice and less than twenty percent actual performance. If we are constantly evaluating our students' use of literacy skills and strategies without practice, their learning is probably superficial at best and could shut down all together.

Make sure your classroom is a place where it is okay to try and try again!

Promote Reading, Writing, Speaking, Listening, and Viewing

This is another area that changes as we get older. Think about it. Primary classrooms are often extremely active and noisy places. One teacher we know says, "Real learning is messy." It requires that the learner is active.

Most intermediate teachers find it easy to give reading and writing practice time. It really requires little effort. But it is easy to omit the speaking, listening, and viewing if we are not careful.

It is easy to fall into the trap of thinking that as students age, the more structured and less action there should be in their classroom. There is no question that they are bigger and often more lanky, so movement can be difficult. It is important, though, that we maintain a healthy balance and promote all aspects of communication in our classes. Literacy is an extremely social process. It requires thinking, reading, writing, looking, considering, and then talking.

Several of the activities in this book encourage students to talk and share their thinking with one or more other students. Help your students know what the expectations are for movement and appropriate noise in your classroom. Be very clear about when it is okay to talk and when it is time to listen. Above all, find ways to incorporate oral language time into the literacy block.

Make sure this focus on reading, writing, and speaking is also meshed with opportunities to listen and view different forms of thinking and learning. Only when we use all these processes will we truly create proficient learners and thinkers.

Investigate Text in a Variety of Genres

Literacy stations provide an opportunity to integrate content area reading. This is also a time to help students explore a variety of genres so that they can make wise book selections. It is always amazing to watch students go into a school media center and select books. Often they have no idea just how to proceed. They don't know how to find books that interest them or that are at an appropriate reading level.

Take the time to introduce a variety of genres at the beginning of the school year and then revisit them throughout the year. Watch for opportunities to celebrate different genres with your read-aloud and whole-group reading sessions. Don't forget to include media like comics, maps, newspapers, and magazines to help students really understand this concept.

Most station activities in this book can be used with either fiction or informational text of any kind. There are activities, however, that are specifically geared toward one or the other. Discuss these special cases when you put one of these activities up for a cycle. Students must select activities for their contract that are appropriate for the anchor text they have chosen. You can check for this during your student conferences on day 1 or day 6 of the two-week rotation.

Build and Extend Vocabulary Knowledge

Isabell Beck, Margaret McKeown, and Linda Kucan (2002) have identified three tiers of vocabulary instruction in their research. The first tier is made up of the most basic words and usually requires little if any direct instruction (e.g., *baby, play, house*). The second tier is comprised of high-frequency words that are found across a variety of texts and situations. These are the words that require the most focused vocabulary instruction. The third tier consists of words that are topic-specific and specialized and are not frequently used in general texts. These words are best taught at the point of need in the context of reading. The goal for all vocabulary instruction is two-fold. Students should first increase the number of words they know and use; then they should extend the depth with which they understand these words.

Reading researcher W. Nagy (2003) notes, "The proportion of difficult words in text is the single most powerful predictor of text difficulty, and a reader's general vocabulary knowledge is the single best predictor of how well that reader can understand text" (p. 1). Exposing students to a wide range of vocabulary is critical to ensure literacy success.

Through the stations in this book, students are invited to think about words they do not know and learn them in the context of reading and writing. The best way to learn vocabulary is to read and use more words. Both the texts that students use and their station discussions will help expand their vocabulary.

Practice and Develop Fluency

Fluency is the bridge between word recognition and comprehension. It is the ability to read accurately and automatically with appropriate rate and prosody (expression and phrasing). Fluent readers can concentrate more on the text's meaning rather than on decoding words. Likewise, less fluent readers often find themselves so focused on decoding words that the meaning of the text is lost.

Fluency is best developed over time and through ample practice with appropriate texts. According to M. Wolf and T. Katzir-Cohen (2001), "After it is fully developed, reading fluency refers to a level of accuracy and rate, where decoding is relatively effortless; where oral reading is smooth and accurate with correct prosody; and where attention can be allocated to comprehension" (p. 219).

Dr. Timothy Rasinski (2003, 2004), a leading reading researcher, notes that there are several ways to help students increase their fluency, such as modeling fluent reading, repeated reading, assisted reading, and choral reading. Rasinski maintains that repeated reading is one of the most effective ways to build a student's oral fluency rate. He suggests that an authentic setting that is inviting to the reader facilitates this acquisition. Rasinski further notes that oral performance of a passage for an audience is the most authentic reason for wanting to engage in repeated readings, or rehearsal.

Research like this is one of the key reasons that we created a station with fluency as the primary focus. Students have the opportunity to develop and practice their fluency in meaningful and enjoyable ways. They will also develop their fluency as they interact with their anchor text and the other readers in the classroom.

Enrich Learning and Comprehension across the Content Areas

We hear teachers complain over and over, "There is no time to teach science or social studies." Certainly the curriculum is more densely packed than ever before. Teachers must, then, find ways to integrate content in meaningful ways throughout the school day.

Our children are being raised in an information age. They have more information at their fingertips today than any previous generation. Rather than mastering discreet content area skills, they must learn how to access, process, and communicate information from a variety of informational text. For a list of station activities that are specifically geared to informational text, see page 189.

Using the literacy station time to help students learn these new skills well will help them when they are required to read and understand key concepts of science and social studies.

Be Open-ended and Engaging

One of the biggest traps for teachers who purchase pre-made station or center activities is that they are often closed-ended, like glorified worksheets. Think about some of the materials that are on the market: match the word with a definition, find all the words that contain a diphthong, or read a predetermined story and answer literal questions about it. These are closed-ended activities. There is nothing inherently wrong with them. However, the practice they provide does not lead to deeper levels of textual understanding. Such activities are often completed in five minutes, and once done, there really isn't much need for revisiting them.

Stations should regenerate themselves. The tasks students are asked to complete should help them delve into the meaning of the text and/or become better readers. Furthermore, completing an activity one time with a text does not have to be the only time. Students can complete the activities again and again because their anchor texts change.

In addition to being open-ended, stations should be engaging. In a speech given at the 2008 *International Reading Association National Conference*, teacher researcher and author Stephanie Harvey said,"If we are teaching kids while they are not engaged, we might as well not be teaching them at all." Missing from many intermediate classrooms is the idea of fun! It is okay to let kids paint, create dramatic retellings, and engage in other fun activities. In fact, the research indicates that readers who are having fun are more likely to retain what they are learning. So don't be afraid to throw a little laughter into the station time. Your students and you will be much happier.

Enable Teacher Assessment and Evaluation of Students' Application of Literacy Skills and Strategies

Earlier we talked about stations being primarily for practice. Clearly understanding this statement is important. Notice that we don't recommend giving a grade. While there may be times that students do earn a grade for their work, most of the work is simply practice and evidence of thinking.

You should consider assessment in the context of your teaching, of course. Seeing what your students know and can do when they are practicing and applying what you have taught them is really important. Are they able to apply the skills in a sensible way? Can they transfer their new knowledge into other texts effectively? Is their thinking deep and meaningful?

Use the station time to observe carefully the work your students are doing. Make notes. Plan your mini-lessons based on what students know and can do and where they need to go next.

Differentiate for Success

Although differentiation is not part of the definition we use for a literacy station, it is a key part of each activity in this book. In general, the activity provides a responsive framework for students. We have included ideas of differentiation that simplify activities for struggling readers and enrich activities for students who are above level.

Carol Tomlinson, the author of *Differentiated Instruction,* notes that "teachers can differentiate at least four classroom elements based on student readiness, interest, or learning profile: (1) content—what the student needs to learn or how the student will get access to the information; (2) process—activities in which the student engages in order to make sense of or master the content; (3) products—culminating projects that ask the student to rehearse, apply, and extend what he or she has learned in a unit; and (4) learning environment—the way the classroom works and feels." During station time, you can differentiate in any of these ways for your students. Differentiation allows us to seek success for each student in our classroom every single day.

One way you may have to differentiate is to freshen up an activity. Occasionally, students may not connect with an activity and become disengaged with the entire process. Sometimes a simple change can make a big difference. For example, rather than drawing a response, we may let students paint one day. Or, they may revisit a former anchor text to complete an activity. Another way to freshen up is actually to introduce some new activities in the stations. You probably have plenty of resources with many great ideas. Consider adding some of these student responses to your stations to change them a bit. You will probably find a whole new level of student enthusiasm.

Chapter 3
Getting Started with Literacy Stations

And You're Off!

Okay, you know what literacy stations are and the importance of implementing them in your classroom. You have decided which stations you want to start with, and you have created some great new materials to help students reinforce literacy skills. You are probably now thinking, how do I move forward with all of these great new tools?

This question is, perhaps, one of the hardest a teacher has to answer when implementing stations. On the following pages, you will find tips both to help you get started and stay organized with station introduction and to help your students develop independent monitoring of their own learning and pacing during literacy station time.

While you may feel an overwhelming urge to share immediately with your students this newfound wealth of activities, we offer one big suggestion: DON'T! The benefit of taking the time to teach and model will far outweigh any mad rush to expose them to a plethora of material all at once. When you begin using stations, only open a few at a time. One hard and steadfast rule we adhere to is that each station and activity must be modeled carefully so students understand the directions and expectations exactly. If you give them too much to remember at once, they will be confused as they move from station to station. Worse, their literacy may not improve, defeating the very goal of station work.

Confusion can lead to two outcomes: First, it may evolve into disengagement of your students. Though trying to complete the task, they may not know exactly WHAT they are supposed to be doing. Second, confusion can also cause students constantly to seek help for clarification and direction. How often in a student conference or a small-group activity do you find individual students approaching you with a cry of, "I don't understand…"? You wonder, "Didn't I already say that?" Do you ever wish you had a built-in tape recorder to hit "Rewind" and "Play," over and over? Maybe your students were just confused from the start.

Carefully consider the goal for this part of your day: You want to be meeting with small guided reading groups during station rotation time, and so you need your students to be as self-sufficient and engaged as possible. They will need to know just what to do in each open station, where to put materials when they are finished, and what to do when they are ready to move on. (Further explanation of classroom management during guided reading groups will follow later in this section.) You must establish clear procedures and then practice these procedures. A rule of thumb: model, model, model. Modeling lets your students know just what you want and expect from them during station cycle time.

Start off S-L-O-W-L-Y!

You have probably heard the old saying about eating an elephant: "One bite at a time,"right? A great way to begin station implementation is by introducing just two stations, with one activity each, in the first two-week cycle. While that may not sound like much, having the students become proficient at simply following the procedures for, and thoroughly completing, two station activities independently is an attainable goal. If this goal can be achieved while going through small-group tasks, adding new station activities later on as you incorporate new texts and skills into your program will be much easier.

One of your next questions might be"Which stations should I use in the beginning?" We suggest starting with Reading Response Journals, from the Written Response station (see pages 169 to 176.) Early in the year, we focus intently on reader's workshop mini-lessons that establish procedures and routines for this specific time of day. These lessons are based on the work of Irene Fountas and Gay Su Pinnell in their book, *Guiding Readers and Writers, Grades Three through Six: Teaching Comprehension, Genre, and Content Literacy.* In the reader's workshop section, Fountas and Pinnell have outlined mini-lessons for the first twenty days of school. These mini-lessons are largely geared to readers sustaining themselves in text and establishing and maintaining a Reading Response Journal.

After teaching students to use their journals, we suggest you pick any other station and activity that best suits your students' needs and interests. To develop vocabulary building activities, many teachers select an activity from the Word Work station (Chapter 10). Others, preferring to concentrate immediately on activities that develop comprehension for fiction or non-fiction reading, will choose a station from the Comprehension stations (Chapter 6). The choice is yours. Simply make sure your selection is directly linked to your and your students' needs at the moment.

Whatever stations you choose to use in the beginning, you need to make sure you and your students understand three important elements of the learning cycle: the Literacy Learning Plan, anchor texts, and Table Talks.

The Literacy Learning Plan

The station rotation is designed to last two weeks. Students plan for and design their own learning using the Literacy Learning Plan. We use this plan with the older students who decide what stations they will go to as we monitor their progression throughout the cycle. When you give students ownership of their learning plan, both their interest and the quality of their work increase.

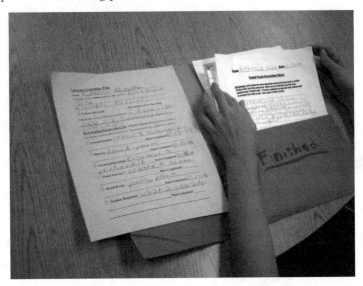

The Literacy Learning Plan serves as a guide for students to use during the two-week cycle. It also allows you to monitor learning and growth of your readers.

Following are two sample Literacy Learning Plans we have used with students. The first contract is the simpler of the two and is good to use with younger students or at the beginning of station use. The second contract is more detailed and includes an opportunity for students to explain how they will demonstrate their learning in each of the stations. The second plan also includes information about the table talk (explained on page 29). We have found that younger students need a separate form for the Table Talk and have included it on page 24.

Literacy Learning Plan

Name: _____ **Cycle Dates:** _____

⚓ **My anchor text for this cycle is** _____

_____

by_____ .

❏ **I chose this book.**   ❏ **My teacher chose this book.**

I chose this book because _____

✎ **My Learning Plan for this Cycle**—CHECK 4 stations that you plan to complete for this cycle. Then write on the line the activity you have chosen.

❏ **Comprehension:** _____

_____ **Date Completed:** _____

❏ **Fluency:**_____

_____ **Date Completed:** _____

❏ **Listening/Speaking:** _____

_____ **Date Completed:** _____

❏ **Visual Literacy:** _____

_____ **Date Completed:** _____

❏ **Word Work:** _____

_____ **Date Completed:** _____

❏ **Written Response:** _____

_____ **Date Completed:** _____

Literacy Learning Plan

⚓ **Name:** _____ **Cycle Dates:** _____

My anchor text for this cycle is _____

_____

by_____ .

❏ I chose this book.   ❏ My teacher chose this book.

I chose this book because _____

✎ **My Learning Plan for this Cycle**—CHECK 4 stations that you plan to complete for this cycle. Then write on the line the activity you have chosen.

❏ I will demonstrate my **comprehension** by _____

_____ Date Completed: _____

❏ I will practice **written response** by _____

_____ Date Completed: _____

❏ I will enhance my **fluency** by _____

_____ Date Completed: _____

❏ I will practice my **listening and speaking skills** by_____

_____ Date Completed: _____

❏ I will work with **words** by _____

_____ Date Completed: _____

❏ I will demonstrate my **visual literacy** by _____

_____ Date Completed: _____

❏ I will complete my **Table Talk** with _____

_____ Date Completed: _____

Anchor Text

The anchor text is the text a student chooses to use to complete each of his or her learning station activities and the Table Talk during a two-week cycle. Once students are able to read, they need to be able to sustain their reading for extended periods of time. Usually, this involves chapter books or longer informational texts. Even sophisticated picture books provide opportunities to reread and comprehend more deeply. Take time in the beginning of the year to introduce the concept of an anchor text to your students.

From Sandy: When introducing anchor text, I have my students visualize a setting:

> Okay boys and girls. Close your eyes. We are getting ready to paint another mental picture. Remember—we call that "visualizing," right? No peeking, so you really can see every part of this scene. Here goes! Imagine you are taking a boat out for a little fishing trip some sunny day. The sky is blue; you can feel the rush of the air as your boat zooms ahead. Up ahead, you and your family think you have found the perfect spot for fishing. You would like to just sit here and enjoy the ocean breeze, casting your lines in the water for hours while you try to lure the fish in. How can you do that? Now, open your eyes and talk to the person sitting next to you.

I allow a few minutes of conversation, and invariably, someone mentions that an anchor can be dropped to stop the boat in its place. While listening to all ideas, I make certain I call upon the student who commented about a boat's anchor. We discuss the fact that an anchor that is dropped from a boat allows that boat not to drift off and keeps the boat on its current course without getting lost.

I then explain that we use one specific title during our station time to help us stay on track with our learning about reading and writing. If we stick to one text, we understand more clearly what we read; we visualize ideas from the passages in the text; we read our favorite parts more fluently. I explain that we will call this one book our "anchor text." Anchor text prevents our reading from drifting away, in the same way that a boat will not drift away if it is properly anchored. I find the students really seem to understand this analogy and grasp the concept of anchor text quickly.

The Literacy Learning Plan includes space for students to record their anchor text. It also asks them to mark whether it was selected by them or the teacher. We believe strongly in student selection of anchor texts in most situations. Students will become more interested in books they have chosen themselves.

However, you may want to use a teacher-selected anchor text when completing station contracts for the first time. In fact, we suggest using a whole-group read-aloud as your anchor text during the very first cycle you complete. Using a common anchor text for all students during this "how-to" period, you can focus on the process of station work and station work folder completion.

Occasionally students may need a little guidance choosing a book that is "just right." You may want the student to pick one of two books you have chosen. This still gives the student some option, but an option controlled by what you know about that student and his or her reading ability.

From Sandy: As an added note: I have had some students complete one week of the two-week rotation and ask to make a new anchor text selection, perhaps due to a returned library book or a finished book they no longer want to work with. They can simply add a number 1 by the first title and then number 2 by a second title they record. Please—be flexible with this form to make it work for you and your students.

Table Talk

A third component of the station time that you and your students must understand is the Table Talk. This component affords students focused time to discuss an anchor text they have been reading with other students. We have included a space to record information about the Table Talk on the detailed Literacy Learning Plan (page 25). But we also use the Table Talk with our younger learners. You can copy a separate Table Talk Log (page 186) and staple it to, or make it the second side of, the simpler Literacy Learning Plan.

In addition to the recording form, a set of Table Talk Guidelines is found in the Resources on page 185. Use these guidelines to help students remember exactly what is expected of them during this activity.

Table Talks can be conducted in several ways. You may simply incorporate them into the station time, when students meet with the student (or students) they have designated as their Table Talk partner(s). Have them each sign and date each other's paper when completed. You can set aside a specific day and time in your reading block for this activity, perhaps Friday, and have all students meet with their Table Talk partners for book sharing. They can sign and date contracts at that time. Students can record their learning and discussion snippets to share with you.

We have also tried to do Table Talks, literally, within the regular classroom table groupings from time to time. The students do not select a partner on their contract that week. Instead, when the time comes for sharing, they just talk with the person across from them. They can also pair up with the person sitting next to them for a book conversation. (Tip: If you complete any type of weekly Reading Log for homework, this is a wonderful way to make it purposeful. Turn the assignment into an engaging and powerful sharing tool rather than just more homework you have to "check-off.") However you choose to implement a Table Talk time, the important goal is to get students talking about their books with each other!

How Do We Move from Place to Place?

Now that you understand the logic of what you should be doing and the importance of starting out slowly, you may wonder, "How can I get them moving from station to station in an orderly fashion?" Yes, we want them to be self-sufficient and not interrupt us as we teach small groups. But these are older kids. Most intermediate students love being older, and they do not want to be treated like the "little kids" any longer. Does this sound familiar? Well, we have come up with a way to give these "older kids" a bit of station responsibility.

For a moment, turn your thoughts from reading to working out and fitness training. Imagine a group of people working out in a gym. Many concentrate on circuit training—time defines what exercise they do and when they move to the next one. Others may stay on a predetermined program of fitness. Still others do what they want when they want to do it. Stations can work the same way. Some students will methodically complete their contracted activities. Others will use their contracts very carefully to determine their plan. And those that pursue their programs more randomly may need to complete part of an activity on one day and finish it the next.

Teachers often use similar procedures when scheduling stations, or as they're often called in primary grades, "center time." In many primary classrooms, the students need more help with the pacing of these rotations. Therefore, the teacher largely controls the movement and choice. These teachers will usually have scheduled lists of which students will go to which centers on which day, and who will move to new ones and at what time. Some signal at specific time intervals when students move to new centers.

All of these strategies for movement between centers or stations can still work with older students. But by intermediate grades, students are really ready to make additional choices themselves. Students can set goals for themselves and monitor their success. When they have choice, there will be depth and complexity added to their work because they will have ownership for the task at hand.

We believe a predetermined "training program" is not best for intermediate kids. If we want them to practice necessary skills—those which we have modeled in whole-group lessons—we need to give them a menu of fun, creative, and open-ended activities from which they can choose. When students choose and plan their learning, great things happen! Choice for us and our students comes in the form of the Literacy Learning Plan.

Introducing and Implementing the Literacy Learning Plan Recipe for Station Success

1. The beginning of the year is the perfect time to introduce your class to the first two stations you have selected. Explain to students that eventually they will have a choice of six total activities within their stations during each two-week cycle. Usually they will complete four activities in each cycle. They will also acquire more freedom of choice as the year progresses and they demonstrate understanding of the work expected of them.

2. Remind students that each two-week cycle centers on an "anchor text." This text may be selected by the teacher, but usually it will be student-selected. The anchor text will be used to complete the station activities throughout the cycle. During this introduction, we suggest using a whole-group read-aloud or shared reading selection as the whole-group anchor text.

3. Tell students that they will each develop a Literacy Learning Plan, or a contract of work to complete during the two-week cycle. Even if you are not pulling small groups yet, students can practice completing and implementing their Literacy Learning Plan for the two station activities you have selected for practice. Before they practice, model correct ways to fill out the plan.

4. Remember to discuss how and when to move from station to station, where to put completed work, and when to meet for reading group. Plan how and where you want students to store their in-process and completed work. We find that a student work folder works well. You may, however, want to use a work basket or file in each station.

5. Teach and model what students should do if their station work is completed before the two-week cycle is over. We suggest they start a new book and record their thinking in their reading journal and/or add an additional Table Talk (see page 27). You may also want to provide a chart that represents a list of options titled, "What to Do When You're Finished." (Note: After you have introduced several station activities, you can set up a "free choice" basket. See page 37 for an explanation.)

6. Hold an abbreviated whole-class practice session. Students can practice completing a station activity as you assess individual students for future groupings. Shorten the allotted station time in these initial practices so that you can come back together and reflect on successful strategies and strategies that still need work.

   - Was the noise level acceptable?
   - Was the work quality work?
   - Was there confusion?
   - Were materials used appropriately?

   Setting clear expectations from the beginning will save you and your students headaches later on.

7. Remind students that eventually they will have a wide range of choices for responding to books they read. Each station activity you introduce is designed to help them practice important literacy skills in meaningful ways that they find engaging and fun.

8. When students are comfortable with station procedures and routines for the first two activity choices, repeat these steps as you add more options for them. Gradually introduce each of the six stations with up to two activities for each. Make sure you take the time to introduce all six stations: Comprehension, Fluency, Listening and Speaking, Visual Literacy, Word Work, and Written Response.

9. By starting with just a few stations and activities, you can familiarize students to the routines of station time and your guided reading group procedures. You can also get initial and often time-consuming assessments done. With the assessment done, your students will be trained and ready to go. It's a win-win situation!

To further extend the learning and develop an understanding of stations, have students brainstorm ideas about the importance of each area and the literacy concept it represents. You will be surprised with some of their responses! Record their thinking on chart paper and post it in or near the station. If they take some ownership in knowing what these literacy concepts are, they will be more aware as they develop intellectually.

Once students know the procedures and routines for the two-week cycle, plan to introduce at least one activity per station during each cycle throughout the year. The ultimate goal is to have several activities for each of the six stations for students to use during each cycle. Thus, you will not have to create and introduce new activities constantly, and your students will have enough choices to sustain them for several literacy cycles.

From Sandy: I like to give my students two activities per station to develop their Literacy Learning Plan. Once students are familiar with a specific activity and I'm ready to add a new one to the station, I like to create a free choice file. Students know they can go to these activities if they complete their contracted cycle work before the end of the cycle. (See page 37 for more on free choice files.)

Students will eventually select one activity from four of the six stations to demonstrate their understanding of the anchor text, which helps students succeed. You may also choose to have students complete six activities (one per station) over the two-week cycle. The activities students are completing should be primarily for practice. Students should never be left to work on new skills or new content independently. When thinking about literacy acquisition, the old adage is true: "Practice makes perfect!"

Chapter 4

Planning and Establishing the Literacy Learning Cycle

After all six stations are ready to open simultaneously, you will need to plan and introduce activities for each new cycle. Suggested steps for this introduction follow:

1. Select each cycle's station activities based on the needs of your students and your current teaching focus. Remember it is okay to have a couple of activities in each station for students if your students know and understand how to make choices.

2. Hold a whole-group meeting. Give your students a brief synopsis of or introduction to each open station and activity for the cycle. Have all activity choices posted for easy viewing. Full-color reproducibles of the literacy station headings and activity titles are available for download at www.maupinhouse.com/pdf/IntermediateLiteracyStations.zip. Laminate these and use on a pocket chart to display options. This is an easy and colorful way to explain the options for the cycle. Furthermore, the chart is always posted for any student who needs a reminder of what the open stations are!

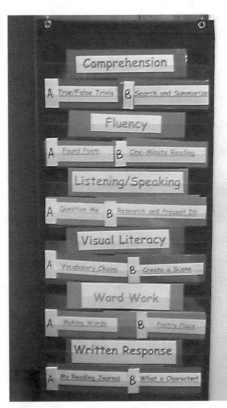

From Sandy: I keep all of the individual activity titles that are not currently in use hidden underneath the actual literacy station heading title on my pocket chart. That way, when I want to change one, they are there, already laminated and available for an easy switch out.

Day 1

3. Once students know the activities from which to choose, have them use independent reading time on day 1 to select their anchor text, take time to read it, reflect on it, and complete their Literacy Learning Plan.

4. Remind students they need to select and complete four of the six station activities before the end of the two-week rotation. Be sure to discuss the idea that they are setting goals for themselves for this period of time, and that they should be choosing activities that allow them to complete quality work. The two-week period is long enough to complete the required station work and to be pulled for small-group reading several times.

Days 2-5

5. During days 2-5 of the two-week cycle, you will continue meeting with your reading groups, and students will complete their station work. Because they are self-paced and have made their own learning plan, they will move to new station activities when appropriate. No specific rotation plan or schedule is in place.

   If you have chosen to make the station a physical location, you may need to establish guidelines regulating the number of students in one station at one time. Generally, students are free to move about in order to complete their plans accordingly. This freedom, or choice, will allow them to get their tasks done with peers of their choosing. You may want to remind them that by the final day of the contract, all station activities must be satisfactorily completed. With occasional reminders, this plan is very successful, and the students enjoy the ownership of this process.

Day 6

6. On day 6, conduct mini-conferences during the reading workshop time to see how students are moving through their station contracts and to ensure that the anchor text is an appropriate match for each student. This is a good time to give gentle reminders and help any student who may need redirection. You may also want to help students plan ahead by thinking about the next cycle.

Days 7-10

7. On days 7-10, students continue to move through their station contracts as you conduct small guided reading groups and/or reading conferences.

The table on the next page shows a possible schedule for reading workshop with literacy stations. It also allows you to see how the days of a typical two-week cycle flow.

Day 1	Introduce any new stations through shared or guided experiences
	Use independent reading time to access and comprehend texts in preparation for stations. After reading, students develop their personal plan for response and further reading over the next nine days. In addition to their stations, all students must sign up for a Table Talk time to take place at least once during the ten-day rotation.
	The teacher can work on individual reading records or progress monitoring during this time.
Days 2-5	Students begin to implement their personal station plan during the workshop time.
	The teacher pulls two to three guided reading groups daily.
Day 6	Through two-minute individual conferences, the teacher monitors progress of each student's plan.
	Students have sustained independent reading time. They continue with or modify their plan based on their reading and conference time.
Days 7-10	Students continue their station plan during workshop time.
	The teacher pulls two to three guided reading groups for instruction and/or intervention daily.

Managing Station Activities

Once your stations are up and running and your students are comfortable with setting bi-weekly goals for their literacy learning time, you are ready to give them even more choices. We like to offer two choices in each of the six stations for the entire cycle. We label these choices A and B.

The only difference in the introduction and implementation of the two-week cycle is that in each new cycle, within each station, the most recently introduced activity is retained as choice B, and a new activity is introduced as choice A for that cycle. Students still use their Day 1 reflection time to complete a Literacy Learning Plan, but now they will have twelve total activities to use in planning. You may also want to add a third activity choice to each station, based on your comfort level and the familiarity your students have with each activity.

On page 35 you will find a Station Rotation Table that uses the activities in this book. This plan covers six cycles (or twelve weeks). It provides a rotation of activities that are possible once students are familiar with the procedures. Because students are constantly using new anchor texts to explore the literacy stations, having just a few activities while maintaining interest in the classroom is possible. The same activity will look very different with new text.

When students are looking for fresh ideas, ask them to share suggestions for added activities or changes to existing activities. Student ideas are often simple and easy to implement. And when they come up with them, the ownership for stations and literacy increases ten-fold!

From Susan: If your students come up with a new twist on an activity, have them write it on a sticky note and adhere it to the directions. Make sure you write "This idea is from (<u>name</u>)." or "Thank you for this idea, (<u>name</u>)!" on the note. Imagine students' delight when they get to be such an integral part of the learning that takes place in your classroom!

Station Rotation Table: 12 Weeks of Station Activity Plans

Station	Cycle 1	Cycle 2	Cycle 3	Cycle 4	Cycle 5	Cycle 6
Comprehension	*Search and Summarize *Senses Brainstorm	*Senses Brainstorm *True/False Trivia	*True/False Trivia *Let's Take a Trip	*Let's Take a Trip *Author's Study	*Author's Study *Senses Brainstorm	*Senses Brainstorm *Search and Summarize
Written Response	*My Reading Journal *Nose for News	*Nose for News *Dig Deeper	*Dig Deeper *What a Character!	*What a Character! *Create-a-Story	*Create-a-Story *My Reading Journal	*My Reading Journal *Dig Deeper
Fluency	*Little Buddy *Found Poem	*Found Poem *Reader's Theater	*Reader's Theater *One-Minute Reading	*One-Minute Reading *Recording Studio	*Recording Studio *Little Buddy	*Little Buddy *One-Minute Reading
Listening and Speaking	*Computer Presentation *Merry-Go-Round	*Merry-Go-Round *Question Me	*Question Me *Research and Present It	*Research and Present It *Karaoke	*Karaoke *Question Me	*Question Me *Merry-Go-Round
Word Work	*Poetry Place *Making Words	*Making Words *Prefix/Suffix Word Play	*Prefix/Suffix Word Play *Grab a Word, Make a Sentence	*Grab a Word, Make a Sentence *Word Gathering	*Word Gathering *Poetry Place	*Poetry Place *Prefix/Suffix Word Play
Visual Literacy	*Create a Scene *Vocabulary Chains	*Vocabulary Chains *Food for Thought	*Food for Thought *Create-a-Model	*Create-a-Model *Vocabulary Word Art	*Vocabulary Word Art *Food for Thought	*Food for Thought *Create a Scene
Free Choice	*True/False Trivia *What a Character! *Recording Studio *Question Me *Word Gathering *Food for Thought	*Author's Study *Create-a-Story *Little Buddy *Karaoke *Grab a Word, Make a Sentence *Create a Scene	*Senses Brainstorm *Nose for News *Found Poem *Computer Presentation *Making Words *Vocabulary Chains	*Search and Summarize *My Reading Journal *Reader's Theater *Merry-Go-Round *Poetry Place *Food for Thought	*Let's Take a Trip *Dig Deeper *One-Minute Reading *Research and Present It *Prefix/Suffix Word Play *Create-a-Model	*True/False Trivia *Create-a-Story *Reader's Theater *Computer Presentation *Making Words *Vocabulary Chains

Chapter 5
More Ideas for Station Management and Planning

No doubt you will have days when you will want to put up a host of board assignments, hand out a bunch of worksheets, and have students sit in their desks quietly so you can teach. We all do. At those times—when we are ready to throw in the literacy station towel—the wise teacher steps back and asks "What is happening here?" Chances are, most issues that arise will have to do with management or planning. Sometimes we plan too much for our students. Other times, we don't plan enough. Still at other times, the placement of a station or the material within that station is the problem. This chapter will give you some further ideas for classroom and station management and planning.

Free Choice Station Files

What do your students do when they are done with their contracts and the two weeks are not over? Chatting with a neighbor about the baseball game or the latest movie probably is not high on your list, so arm yourself with a bag of tricks. All you need to do is find a box, a crate, or some other container to house familiar activity folders and envelopes. You could use a separate colored hanging file for each different station theme. Or you could use a different colored basket for each one.

Once you have housed the materials, show your students where familiar activities that are not in the current rotation will be kept: the Free Choice stations. When their contracted station work and their Table Talk is completed and turned in, they may go to any free choice activity they wish for further reinforcement and practice.

The beauty of this plan is that as new activities are introduced and old ones are removed, the "old ones" suddenly become free choices! Your file of readily available, hands-on, literacy-rich activities is at arm's reach at all times when students need supplemental work. You don't have to create new activities all the time. In fact, we find that the thirty station activities in this book can sustain our intermediate students for an entire year! The best part of all is that they already know the directions because they have previously been in stations for four weeks. What a bargain!

The other option available when contract work is completed is sustained silent reading, or SSR. (Some teachers may call this D.E.A.R. time: drop everything and read.) Perhaps you and your students could develop your own unique acronym for silent reading time!

Week-to-Week Lesson Planning

Once you are off and running, and have plenty of activities to add to your bi-weekly rotations, you may have a difficult time figuring out which activities to include for your students to practice. You may also have a hard time keeping track of what you have already practiced and what you will do next. On the following page, you will find a lesson planning template. Use this to keep track of the activities you have introduced and make notes as to how to modify the next use of the activity.

When planning your lessons, choose those that are going to help develop the skills and strategies you are using in your whole and small-group lessons. Keep in mind, that those "favorite activities" of your students can be modified with different texts multiple times to meet many different needs.

Two sample lesson templates follow. The first blank template has the six literacy stations with space for the recording of one activity. If it is early in the year and you are only using two, three, or four stations, just record whatever information you need in those open stations and either leave blank or write "omit" in the others.

The second blank template is used when your class progresses to the point of being able to handle more choices of activities within all six stations.

Following the lesson planning template on page 39 is a completed lesson plan template. It shows each literacy station at mid-year when students are given a choice of two activities at each station. At this time, they consider all available activities and select the four they most want to practice.

Sample Lesson Plan Template for Literacy Stations—One Station per Literacy Focus Area

Time Frame: **/**/** to **/**/**		
Literacy Stations	**Due Dates:**	**Notes/Observations to Make:**
1. Comprehension Materials: (Circle One) Introduce/Revisit ESOL/ESE Code(s):	DUE **/**/**	NOTE: Students turn this paper in with their work at the end of the literacy station cycle.
2. Written Response Materials: (Circle One) Introduce/Revisit ESOL/ESE Code(s):	DUE **/**/**	
3. Fluency Materials: (Circle One) Introduce/Revisit ESOL/ESE Code(s):	DUE **/**/**	
4. Listening Materials: (Circle One) Introduce/Revisit ESOL/ESE Code(s):	DUE **/**/**	
5. Word Work Materials: (Circle One) Introduce/Revisit ESOL/ESE Code(s):	DUE **/**/**	
6. Visual Literacy Materials: (Circle One) Introduce/Revisit ESOL/ESE Code(s):	DUE **/**/**	

Sample Lesson Plan Template for Literacy Stations—Two Stations per Literacy Focus Area to Offer Students More Choices When They Become Proficient with the Station Process

Time Frame: **/**/** to **/**/**		
Literacy Stations NOTE: Students turn this paper in with their work at the end of the literacy station cycle.	**Due Dates:**	**Notes/Observations to Make:**
1. Comprehension—CHOOSE BETWEEN: A) _____ Materials: B) _____ Materials: (Circle One) Introduce/Revisit ESOL/ESE Code(s):	DUE **/**/**	Either station may be selected and contracted for during this two-week station cycle.
2. Written Response—CHOOSE BETWEEN: A) _____ Materials: B) _____ Materials: (Circle One) Introduce/Revisit ESOL/ESE Code(s):	DUE **/**/**	Either station may be selected and contracted for during this two-week station cycle.
3. Fluency—CHOOSE BETWEEN: A) _____ Materials: B) _____ Materials: (Circle One) Introduce/Revisit ESOL/ESE Code(s):	DUE **/**/**	Either station may be selected and contracted for during this two-week station cycle.

4. Listening/Speaking—CHOOSE BETWEEN: A) _____ Materials: B) _____ Materials: (Circle One) Introduce/Revisit ESOL/ESE Code(s):	DUE **/**/**	Either station may be selected and contracted for during this two-week station cycle.
5. Word Work—CHOOSE BETWEEN: A) _____ Materials: B) _____ Materials: (Circle One) Introduce/Revisit ESOL/ESE Code(s):	DUE **/**/**	Either station may be selected and contracted for during this two-week station cycle.
6. Visual Literacy—CHOOSE BETWEEN: A) _____ Materials: B) _____ Materials: (Circle One) Introduce/Revisit ESOL/ESE Code(s):	DUE **/**/**	Either station may be selected and contracted for during this two-week station cycle.

Sample Completed Lesson Plan for Literacy Stations

Time Frame: **/**/** to **/**/**		
Literacy Stations	**Due Dates:**	**Notes/Observations to Make:**
1. Comprehension A) True-False Trivia* Materials: Station materials, sticky notes, non-fiction books for the topic (Lincoln and Washington) Search and Summarize: Skill-Cause & Effect Materials: Station materials, laminated articles and stories, vis-à-vis markers pencils (Circle One) Introduce/Revisit ESOL/ESE Code(s):	*Required Station DUE **/**/**	*A) All students complete this station and turn their work into the station folder. B) This station is a choice for students after all other required and contracted station work for the cycle has been completed.
2. Written Response—CHOOSE BETWEEN: A) Create-a-Story Matrix Materials: Station materials, sticky notes, personal writing folders, paper, pencils B) Reading Response Journals Materials: Reading Response Journals, pencils, SSR books (Circle One) Introduce/Revisit ESOL/ESE Code(s):	DUE **/**/**	Either station may be selected and contracted for during this two-week station cycle.
3. Fluency—CHOOSE BETWEEN: A) Reader's Theater Materials: Station folder, scripts—Add a new script B) One-Minute Reading Materials: Station envelope, stopwatch, pencils, student-selected reading material (Circle One) Introduce/Revisit ESOL/ESE Code(s):	DUE **/**/**	Either station may be selected and contracted for during this two-week station cycle.

4. Listening/Speaking—CHOOSE BETWEEN: A) Question Me Materials: Station folder, student-selected reading materials B) Reading Merry-Go-Round Materials: Station folder, student-selected reading materials (Circle One) Introduce/Revisit ESOL/ESE Code(s):	DUE **/**/**	Either station may be selected and contracted for during this two-week station cycle.
5. Word Work—CHOOSE BETWEEN: A) Grab A Word, Make A Sentence Materials: Station envelope, paper, pencils B) Gathering Words Materials: Station folder, student-selected reading material (Circle One) Introduce/Revisit ESOL/ESE Code(s):	DUE **/**/**	Either station may be selected and contracted for during this two-week station cycle.
6. Visual Literacy—CHOOSE BETWEEN: A) Vocabulary Chains Materials: Station envelope, construction paper, pencils and markers, glue, tape, or staples B) Food for Thought Materials: Station folder, laminated food packages, paper, pencils Circle One) Introduce/Revisit ESOL/ESE Code(s):	DUE **/**/**	Either station may be selected and contracted for during this two-week station cycle.

From Sandy: In the completed sample, under the Comprehension station, the True-False Trivia activity has an asterisk by it. The plan explains that the asterisk means "required station." There may be times when you are focusing on a specific skill and you want all students to complete a specified activity during the two-week cycle. This is fine. Have your students record this as one of their four choices. They would then select three additional choices independently.

One word of caution, however: Try not to make too many required stations. Assuring that all students practice with a specific skill is important, but the freedom and autonomy of this process is equally important. In many cases, students will complete their contracted activities successfully, with enough time to spare so that they can go to Free Choice stations and get further reinforcement in other skills.

Keep Them on Track
Following the Rules

As we have noted several times, you will want to make sure you have established clear rules and expectations for station work. For some of us it is hard to let go of the idea of controlling what students do and when they do it. However, we want them to have this new autonomy, right? Your letting go of the need to control station time helps give your students ownership in their own learning process. In our classrooms, they are free to move as they choose, provided their work is completed successfully and they remain focused. To help them, we create some simple boundaries:

- There can be no more than four people in a station at one time.
- All voices must be no higher than a "buzz" when station conversation is taking place.
- Have each station cleaned and ready for new learners before going to a new station.
- Respect all opinions and work.
- Only interrupt the teacher for the 3 Bs.

The reasons for such rules are fairly self-explanatory. You must set limits for

1. numbers in each station
2. voice volume
3. cleanup
4. mutual respect and courtesy always

From Sandy: The "3 Bs" rule was created out of a need to keep interruptions minimal for me. Basically, I needed a "rule" to keep students from interrupting me while I was teaching small groups. This is precious and sacred time. Some teachers use a signal, such as a stop sign. If the stop sign is turned around to "STOP," there can be no interruptions. Others wear a special hat that signals the children that they cannot interrupt when it is being worn. While I like signals such as these, I still wanted to allow my students to be able to interrupt for actual emergencies. I came up with the "3 Bs." They can interrupt me for any of the following reasons:

1) If there is any *blood*
2) If there is any *breakage* (any person or any thing)
3) If someone is about to *barf*

I know that may sound a little rough around the edges, but it gets a chuckle from the students when I explain it, which makes it stick! I keep a sign near my small-group area so I can point to remind students to think first before they interrupt. If I get a rush of students coming to me in the middle of reading group time, the students are very quick to ask, "Is this a 3 Bs issue?" They can learn to help one another or become problem solvers on their own in most cases when the answer is a clear "no."

Another simple rule that may be helpful is "Ask three before me." (Some teachers may find this a little more palatable than the 3 Bs!) We have included both an "Is this a 3B issue?" and an "Ask 3 before me!" sign in the Resources on pages 187 and 188 for your use. Feel free to select one of these, or get creative and develop a slogan of your own to signal no interruptions.

The other strategy that helps with management is to have students work in cooperative groups. Our students do this routinely during the school day, so this is quite comfortable for them. If your students are unfamiliar or new to any type of partner or group activities, try to develop some techniques that they can use initially with your guidance and then can transfer to station activities independently. Relying on peers for assistance, feedback, and sharing opportunities are powerful components of our literacy stations. Sometimes we find they are better teachers than we are! This give and take of oral communication further enhances speaking and listening literacy skills, as well as fluency.

How to Keep Track of It All
Student Station Work Folders

When station work begins in the classroom, teachers often ask for easy management so students can be successful with the tasks we ask them to complete. Isn't that what we are all after when implementing a new program? After trying different management systems, this one has proven to be simple and systematic, allowing both teachers and students to keep track of their Literacy Learning Plans and the corresponding activities that accompany the student's individual contracted selections for each two-week cycle. Helping students stay organized is always a good thing!

Each student will need to create a Student Station Work Folder. We use a basic two-pocket folder, which can be plain or wildly decorated. Have students decorate the outside of a plain colored folder with each of the literacy focus areas in crazy fonts. A little fun and creativity can make this folder truly special and personalize it for your students. Students will keep their Literacy Learning Plans in this folder, along with all work in progress.

At the end of the two-week cycle, collect the contract and all activities completed to check on student success. You can have students staple any written activities to the contract for ease of storage. These collections can be saved in a student's individual file for future conferencing with both the student and parents. Finished work can also serve as assessments of whether specific skills have been mastered or need further reinforcement. You may find that you are able to recreate your small groups using student work samples. For example, if you have several students who don't understand summarizing, you could create a small group that focuses on that skill for a period of time. Additionally, you may find that you want to pull a station activity to work on the skill from a different angle during the next cycle.

PART TWO

The Stations, Strategies, And Activities

Chapter 6
Comprehension

Why do you read? The real purpose of reading is to make connections between what you read—the text—and what you already know—your schema. We want our students to be able to truly understand text—to perceive and really grab hold of the ideas they read about. However, reading isn't just something that happens; you really need to think about it. There are seven key components of comprehension that foster the ties between reading and thinking: using schema, predicting/inferring, monitoring, questioning, determining importance, visualizing, and synthesizing/summarizing. The literacy stations in this section touch directly on four of these components: using schema, monitoring, determining importance, and synthesizing/summarizing. However, those components that are not covered here are addressed in other stations throughout this text.

Comprehension is a common thread that links all themes of reading together. Enjoy these activities as you help your students become better readers and thinkers!

Pages	Activity Name	Strategy Focus
50-53	Author's Study	Compare and contrast
54-57	Let's Take a Trip	Monitoring understanding; Finding details to respond to questions in informational text
58-60	Search and Summarize	Locating teacher-designated Target Skill® in fiction or non-fiction text; Writing concise summaries
61-64	Senses Brainstorm	Making connections using schema; Relating to characters in text
65-68	True/False Trivia	Finding relevant and useful information; Using details to determine fact vs. opinion

Literacy Station: Comprehension
Activity: Author's Study

Strategy Focus: Compare and Contrast

Materials: Student-selected books (two by the same author), and the following: one set of directions (p. 52), a cover (p. 51), one Author's Study Response Sheet per student (p. 53), 10" x 13" manila envelope

Preparing the Station:

1. Glue the cover from page 51 to the front of a large manila envelope. Glue the student directions from page 52 to the back of the manila envelope. Laminate.
2. Put the Author's Study Response Sheets inside the manila envelope.

Activity Introduction:

1. Introduce an Author's Study by reading several books by the same author during read-aloud with your students. This allows you to model just what you expect of them from this station activity.
2. Provide plenty of repeated practice comparing and contrasting text and characters, so students are comfortable with that as an independent activity. If yours have not had that prior exposure, we suggest some lessons in that skill before introducing this station.
3. Once you've built prior knowledge, you are ready to explain the activity directions to your students and clarify any questions they may have. Show models of what you expect.

From Sandy: I actually have a model of our class's shared compare/contrast laminated and keep it on display in the station when they are doing Author's Study.

Differentiation for All Students:

1. Guide less confident readers by reading one book together in a reading group and then having them read another by the same author independently. Additionally, several students could be assigned the same title for the independent book, so there will be peers with whom they can discuss the similarities and differences before writing about their reading.
2. Advanced-level learners can add the challenge of a three-title comparison by the same author. I have had students who get very involved in this.

From Sandy: This activity can take longer than the two-week cycle. I tend to grant flexibility when it comes to this kind of eagerness.

Author's Study

Author's Study

Directions:

1. Choose a favorite author of yours.

2. Read one book by that author.

3. Fill out the information about **Book 1** on the **Author's Study Response Sheet**.

4. Read another book by that author.

5. Fill out the information about **Book 2** on the **Author's Study Response Sheet**.

6. Pause to think and reflect how these two books by the same author are alike or different.

7. Write your thoughts about this on the **Compare and Contrast** section of the Author's Study Response Sheet.

8. Put your paper in your Station Work Folder.

Name_____ Date_____

Author's Study

Book 1 Information:

Title: _____

Setting: _____

Main Characters: _____

_____

Book Summary of key events and problem/solution:

_____

_____

_____

_____

_____

_____

Book 2 Information:

Title: _____

Setting: _____

Main Characters: _____

_____

Book Summary of key events and problem/solution:

_____

_____

_____

_____

_____

_____

Compare and Contrast: Tell how this author's books are alike or different:

_____

_____

_____

_____

_____

Literacy Station: Comprehension
Activity: Let's Take a Trip!

Strategy Focus: Monitor understanding; Find details to respond to questions in informational text

Materials: Two file folders of the same color; vellum paper to create pockets; travel brochures; notebook paper and pencils for student use; cover, page 55

Preparing the Station:

1. Glue two file folders together, so that the right side of one overlaps the left side of the other. This will create a tri-fold station folder.
2. Glue the student directions and questions, page 56, to the inside of this folder on the left flap.
3. Create two vellum paper pockets large enough to hold travel brochures, and glue one to the middle section and the other to the right flap. Use these to store several different brochures from your area.
4. On each pocket, glue a label from page 57, "Travel Brochure Pocket."
5. Glue the cover, page 55, to the outside station of the folder. Now laminate for durability. You will need to carefully cut the tops of the pockets to be able to insert your brochures.

Activity Introduction:

1. This station activity can be used as a follow-up after lessons on using directions and basic map reading skills. Practice reading informational text in whole group settings beforehand so students can be comfortable using these materials independently.
2. Explain the student station directions to the class as a whole group. Clarify any questions students may have.
3. You can create great variety with this station simply by altering the travel brochures you put into the pockets.
4. Challenge: Have students choose a character from their anchor text and write about the character visiting the attraction they chose. They can also choose an appropriate setting from the anchor text and create an attraction for that place.

Differentiation for All Students:

1. Pair less confident readers with more fluent readers. These types of reading materials will not be easily modified, so give students the additional support they may require. You can also modify the number of questions they need to respond to for a completed assignment.
2. More advanced readers may want to write additional questions on index cards to put in a separate box labeled "Question Bank." Students can be directed to try these as challenge questions once their assignment is complete.

Let's Take a Trip!

Let's Take a Trip!

Directions:

1. Choose a travel brochure. Write the name of the tourist attraction at the top of your paper.

2. Answer each of the following questions using complete sentences.

3. Put your finished paper in your Station Work Folder.

Questions:

1. Give directions telling how to get to this attraction from your city and state: _____

   _____

   _____

2. Where can you buy food or souvenirs at this tourist attraction? What might you buy there?

3. Can you become a member of this place? If so, how much does membership cost and what are the benefits for joining? If not, tell any ways you can get a discount to save some money here.

4. Name and describe five different attractions, shows, or events to see at this site.

5. What days of the year is this site open to the public and what are the hours? When is it closed?

6. How can you contact this place to obtain more information?

Use these for labels on the pockets to house the cycle's brochures.

Travel
Brochure
Pocket

Travel
Brochure
Pocket

Literacy Station: Comprehension
Activity: Search and Summarize

Strategy Focus: Locate specific Target Skill in fiction or non-fiction text; Write concise summaries

Materials: File folder; fiction and non-fiction passages of one to two pages in length of grade-level appropriate material; construction paper; vis-à-vis markers; paper and pencils

Preparing the Station:

1. Glue the student direction page (60) on the opened file folder. Glue page 59 to the front as a cover. Laminate (opened flat) for durability.

2. Glue each fiction and non-fiction passage onto construction paper, then laminate so that it will create a wipe off surface on each one.

3. Put vis-à-vis markers, paper, and pencil in the station with the file folder and the laminated passages.

Activity Introduction:

1. This station is designed to have students practice several skills: summarizing passages and reviewing a specific Target Skill that you have discussed recently in shared reading and writing experiences. (These can be changed every ten-day rotation, or with any other convenient schedule that best suits your students' learning needs.) Make sure you conduct lessons on summarizing before introducing this station to your students.

2. Write the current Target Skill in the box on the student direction sheet. Some sample Target Skills might include: looking for characteristics of the character, finding descriptions of a place, retelling events in the story.

3. Explain the station directions to students.

4. This is an invaluable activity, because while many students may seem to grasp a new Target Skill initially, it is often at a surface level. When students must actually apply this skill to their reading and writing, they are often faced with a challenge. In this station, students will get great practice focusing on searching for Target Skills as they read. Writing concise summaries of the passages they read helps improve students' comprehension.

Differentiation for All Students:

1. Less confident readers will often find success working with a buddy. You may want to pair them up to complete this station, at least initially. Once they develop more confidence in their skills, you can move them away from this support to independent practice.

2. Students who have mastered searching for one Target Skill and can write concise summaries may find it challenging to search for more than one Target Skill at a time.

Search
AND
Summarize

Search AND Summarize

Directions:

1. Choose a laminated story or article to read.

2. Using one of the wipe-off markers in the station, SEARCH for and underline the current Target Skill:

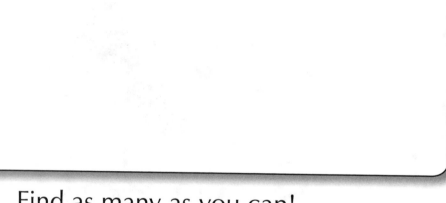

Find as many as you can!

4. Using your own paper, make a list of at least ten of the words or phrases you found.

5. On the same paper, write a three- to four-sentence SUMMARY of the story. Remember, be specific and try to think of the most important details as you write.

6. Keep your paper in your Station Work Folder.

Literacy Station: Comprehension
Activity: Senses Brainstorm

Strategy Focus: Make connections using schema; Relate to characters in text

Materials: Student directions, page 63; student cover, page 62; and record sheet, page 64 (enough copies for your whole class); student-selected books; one 10"x 13" brown envelope

Preparing the Station:

1. Glue the cover from page 62 to the front of a large manila envelope. Glue the student directions from page 63 to the back of the manila envelope. Laminate.
2. Put the student record sheets inside the brown envelope.

Activity Introduction:

1. Most students at this age are quite familiar with their five senses, but it never hurts to do a review of them prior to offering this station activity to students.

From Sandy: One thing I always tell my interns is to never assume they know what you are talking about!

2. Once they are clear about the concepts, you can explain the station directions and clarify any questions that arise.
3. Be sure to let them know the questions on the directions page are guiding questions only. They can choose to respond to other thoughts in each sensory area that may not be listed.

Differentiation for All Students:

1. If you have below-level readers, you may have them choose only a predetermined number of senses to respond to, rather than all five.
2. Cut the cards apart and let struggling readers select two or three to complete the activity.
3. Your advanced readers may have a fun experience turning their five sensory observations into a different writing; try to have them turn as many of their observations as they can into a "sense-adventure" or a sense-themed poem about one of the characters.

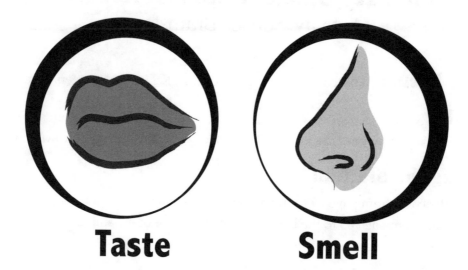

Taste   Smell

Senses Brainstorm

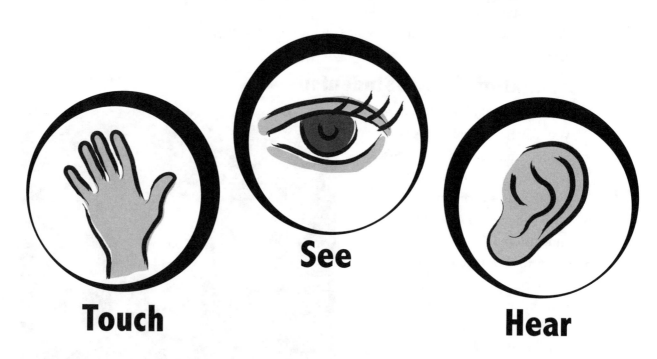

Touch   See   Hear

Senses Brainstorm

1. Read all or part of a book.
2. Think about each of the five senses and the book.
3. Write what you notice about each of the senses in the book.

See

What do the characters see?

Where does the story take place?

What would you see if you visited the place in the book?

What do other characters see?

Hear

What do the characters hear?

What sounds occur during the problem?

What sounds would be in this setting?

Taste

What do the characters taste?

Is there specific food in the story?

Touch

What kind of texture is in the book?

What are some of the things the characters touch?

Are there objects that would be smooth, rough, hard, soft, flat, or bumpy?

Smell

What do the characters smell?

What would you smell if you visited the place in the book?

What do other characters smell?

Senses Brainstorm

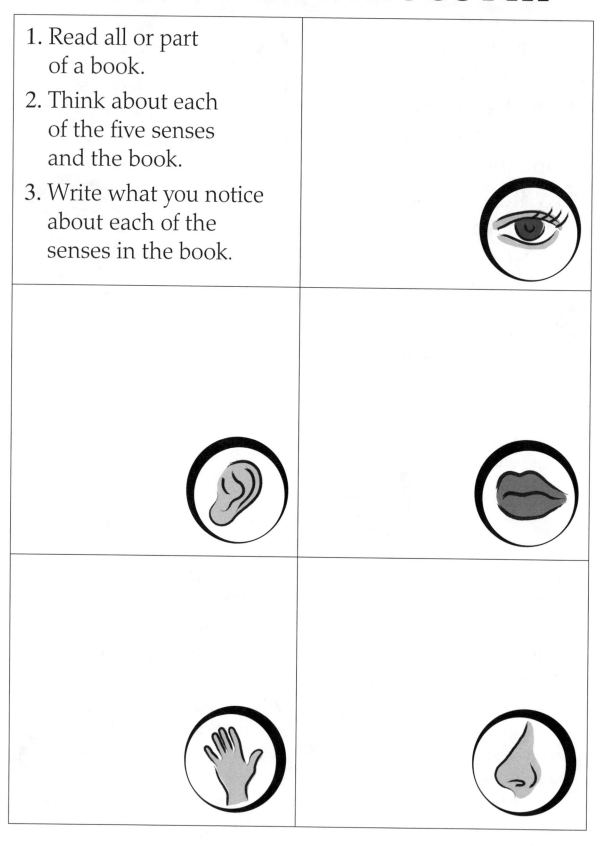

1. Read all or part of a book.

2. Think about each of the five senses and the book.

3. Write what you notice about each of the senses in the book.

Literacy Station: Comprehension
Activity: True/False Trivia!

Strategy Focus: Find relevant and useful information; Use details to determine fact vs. opinion

Materials: Cover, page 66; student directions, page 67; student record sheet, page 68; 3"x 3" sticky notes (six per student); trade books related to a current content theme; markers; pencils

Preparing the Station:

1. Create a model of the student record page, page 68, to display in the station. Adhere six sticky notes to the page in a 2"x 3" grid.
2. Glue the cover from page 66 to the front of a large manila envelope. Glue the student directions from page 67 to the back of the manila envelope. Laminate for durability.
3. Put blank student record sheets and sticky notes inside the envelope. Place markers and pencils at the station for student work materials.
4. Put the content trade books that students will use for the research work of this station in a basket and display at this station.

Activity Introduction:

1. Show students how to set up the paper. Explain the student station directions and clarify any questions.
2. Show them what books they may use. Explain that they can only use these books since partners will be proving one another's written statements either true or false. We all want to have access to the same information for this activity.
3. Once your students understand the process, you can modify it to any content area. It can also be altered to be used for fiction work by having them come up with true and false statements about characters, setting, plot, or problem and solution. You may want to focus the activity on one of these story elements to foster a strong skill base in that area.

Differentiation for All Students:

1. Struggling readers may want to do the statement creation with partners, then switch with another pair to do the proving phase of this activity.
2. Advanced-level readers could choose to create more statements than the required six. They could create a 3"x 3" grid of sticky notes, for example.
3. When two or more students have used the same anchor text, they may complete a True/False Trivia activity using the information from their book.

True/False

Trivia

True/False Trivia

Directions:

1. Take one student record sheet.

2. Put six sticky notes on your paper. Make sure it matches the model. Put two across and three down. (You will have three rows of two when you finish.)

3. Using the station books that are in the basket, read about this week's topic:

   _____.

4. Now you get to write sentences. They can be either TRUE or FALSE. Write a sentence on each sticky note. Under it, write a small T or F so you will know if it is TRUE or FALSE.

5. Find a partner who has also finished this part. Switch response sheets with your partner.

6. Read one another's sentences. Search in the books to decide if the sentence is really TRUE or FALSE. Peek under the sticky note to see if you are correct.

7. If the sentence was FALSE, it is your job to write a sentence under the sticky note that will make it TRUE.

8. Once you and your partner have finished reading each other's papers and making all the sentences TRUE, write both of your names on the backs of both papers and put them in your Station Work Folder.

Name_____Date_____

True/False Trivia Student Response Sheet

Chapter 7
Fluency

Fluent reading is when reading sounds natural, flowing, and the meaning is unbroken. Because fluent readers don't have to worry about decoding words, their attention can be directed to the meaning of what they are reading. Students who are fluent readers also have a stronger self-image and more confidence in public speaking. Unfortunately, for many students, reading fluency is a challenge. We need to give them many opportunities to rehearse and perform readings so that their fluency develops. Remember that the best readers practice a piece several times before the "performance." The Fluency Station offers your students a range of opportunities to practice reading orally, in experiences that vary from independent to partner to small group.

Pages	Activity Name	Strategy Focus
70-73	Found Poem	Adjust reading rate based on purpose, text difficulty, and style
74-77	Little Buddy	Using correct voice variation and expression; Peer relationships
79-82	One-Minute Read	Adjust reading rate based on purpose, text difficulty, and style
83-86	Reader's Theater	Cooperative learning; Using correct voice variation and expression; Oral presentations
87-90	Recording Studio	Demonstrate ability to read on grade level

Literacy Station: Fluency
Activity: Found Poem

Strategy Focus: Adjust reading rate based on purpose, text difficulty, and style

Materials: Cover, page 71; student directions, page 72; Poem Recording Sheet, page 73 (copies for every student in your class); student-selected reading material (fiction or non-fiction); pencils; and one 10"x 13" envelope

Preparing the Station:

1. Glue the cover from page 71 to the front of a large manila envelope. Glue the student directions from page 72 to the back of the manila envelope. Laminate for durability.

2. Store the Poem Recording Sheets in the envelope for student use in the station.

Activity Introduction:

1. This station is effective after you have practiced reading poetry aloud with your students. They must understand the rhythm and language that is often found in poetry. It is also important that students understand that poems don't always rhyme.

2. Model this as a shared writing activity prior to allowing students to create their own Found Poems in the station.

3. Explain the student station directions and clarify any questions.

Differentiation for All Students:

1. Your lower-level readers may have greater success initially by creating a Found Poem with a partner or in a group. After they create their poem together, they can practice reading it in several ways to one another. Once successful, encourage them to attempt a poem independently and then to share their poems with each other.

2. Challenge more confident readers to create a poem from a text in a specific theme. For example, if you are studying the Civil War, provide the students with a basket of books that revolve around that theme. You can get some amazing Found Poems for students to share and discuss. They can compare and contrast the use of details and concepts in their work. Artistic representations can also be added.

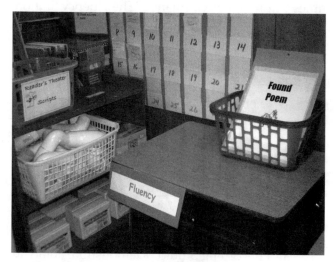

Found
Poem

Found Poem

Directions:

1. Choose a book or article.

2. Find a favorite section of this book or article to read.

3. Use a Poem Recording Sheet to write down the most important words from that section in the order that they appeared. This is your "Found Poem." You should have to add very few, if any, words to your poem.

4. Practice reading this poem to yourself with rhythm. You may want to try it different ways until it sounds "just right" to you.

5. Share your "Found Poem" with someone else in the room.

6. Keep your Poem Recording Sheet in your Station Work Folder.

Name_____**Date**_____

Found Poem
Recording Sheet

<u>Directions:</u> Write down the most important words from your book or article in the order that they appeared. When you are finished, you will have written your "Found Poem." Practice reading it to yourself with rhythm until it sounds just right to you, then share it with a friend.

Literacy Station: Fluency
Activity: Little Buddy

Strategy Focus: Use correct voice variation and expression; Develop peer relationships

Materials: Student directions, cover, and Little Buddy Notes (enough for all students), pages 76-77; a 10"x 13" brown envelope; reading books for a younger class of students

Preparing the Station:

1. Glue the cover on page 76 to the front of a 10"x 13" brown envelope. Glue the directions from page 77 to the back of the envelope. Laminate for durability.

2. Find a class of younger students to be your "Book Buddies." Decide what day will be convenient for your students to read together. Record the buddy class name and the day on the direction page.

3. Have the Little Buddy Notes copied and cut so your students can write a kind note to their buddy after the reading experience.

4. Set the basket of primary level reading books in the station for students to practice with during station time.

Activity Introduction:

1. Explain that they can use any book in the primary basket for this purpose. While it may not be a "just right" book for their present reading level, they will be reading to a younger child. Remind students they need to be very clear and accurate readers to model for younger readers. Encourage the use of voice inflections for different characters, good expression, and fluidity in their reading as they practice.

2. While intermediate students may see it as reading easy books, they have an opportunity to concentrate on those many attributes of oral reading that they sometimes forget when struggling with more challenging text. The other huge benefit is watching them become little teachers.

From Sandy: The pride I see every time my students participate in this is just amazing. If you have never attempted this type of activity, this may be a way to give it a try.

Differentiation for All Students:

1. Pair your most struggling readers with the most emergent readers in the buddy class. Try to work with the other teacher involved to let your lower readers be matched with someone else at a similar level in his or her class. The sudden power less-confident readers feel at being able to help a younger child read, possibly when they have seen themselves as a poor reader for so long, is enormous.

1. Advanced-level readers may be able to have several books prepared to read to their Little Buddy. Encourage them to help the younger child read along on a second read, or even ask some basic questions about simple story elements.

1. It is also fun to let students read an excerpt from their anchor text when it's appropriate for the younger reader. You may encourage this through the weekly reading conference. (Note: Occasionally a student may want to share a portion of his or her anchor text with their little buddy. Have them ok this with you first.)

Little Buddy

Little Buddy

Directions:

1. Choose a book that you would like
   to read aloud to a younger student in
   _____'s class.

2. Practice the book repeatedly so you can read
   it comfortably and with good expression and
   feeling.

3. Be ready to read to your buddy on
   _____.

4. After you have read with your Little Buddy,
   take a note from the envelope to write a note
   to him or her saying what you enjoyed about
   your reading time.

Little Buddy Note

Hi Buddy! I enjoyed spending time reading with you today. The part I liked the best was

_____
_____
_____
_____
_____
_____
_____

Your Friend,

Little Buddy Note

Hi Buddy! I enjoyed spending time reading with you today. The part I liked the best was

_____
_____
_____
_____
_____
_____
_____

Your Friend,

Little Buddy Note

Hi Buddy! I enjoyed spending time reading with you today. The part I liked the best was

_____
_____
_____
_____
_____
_____
_____

Your Friend,

Little Buddy Note

Hi Buddy! I enjoyed spending time reading with you today. The part I liked the best was

_____
_____
_____
_____
_____
_____
_____

Your Friend,

Literacy Station: Fluency
Activity: One-Minute Read

Strategy Focus: Adjust reading rate based on purpose, text difficulty, and style

Materials: Cover, page 80; student directions, page 81; Word Count Record Sheets, page 82 (copied, cut in half so there are enough for each of your students to have one); one 10"x 13" manila envelope; stopwatch

Preparing the Station:

1. Glue the cover from page 80 to the front of a large manila envelope. Glue the student directions from page 81 to the back of the manila envelope. Laminate.

2. Cut the Word Count Record Sheets in half. Keep in the brown envelope for student use in the station.

3. Keep a stopwatch in the brown envelope for students to time themselves during this activity.

Activity Introduction:

1. You will need to instruct your students in how to use a stopwatch prior to having them begin this task independently in stations. We recommend a mini-lesson with either the whole class or small groups for this purpose.

2. Explain that they can use any book they are currently reading to practice reading and to develop their fluency. It is best to use a familiar piece from the anchor text for the cycle.

3. Explain the student station directions and clarify any questions.

Differentiation for All Students:

1. Be sure your students are using text that is familiar and within their independent level of reading. If they choose text that is too challenging, they will only become more frustrated. This is something you hope to avoid with any reader, but especially your struggling readers.

2. Encouraging advanced readers to choose appropriately leveled material to practice and build fluency and challenge them to set a goal for themselves for the second read. They may want to give themselves a self-evaluation on the experience and set a new goal for the next time they practice for fluency.

3. Some readers are very competitive and believe that reading "the most" words in one minute is the goal. This is not so. Remind students that the goal is to read so that someone else can understand the passage when it is read aloud.

One-Minute Reading

One-Minute Reading

Directions:

1. Find a partner to work with.

2. Each of you needs to get a book you can read well. This could be your anchor text or perhaps a class reading selection.

3. Find a stopwatch inside the envelope.

4. Each partner needs to take a Word Count Record Sheet and fill out the top information.

5. Have one partner time the other one reading for one minute, using the stopwatch.

6. Count and record the number of words you read in the one minute. Repeat and see if you can read more words the second time.

7. Switch roles with your partner.

8. Keep your Word Count Record Sheets in your Station Work Folder.

One-Minute Reading Word Count Record Sheet

Name _____

Book or Text Title _____

One- Minute Read #1 Word Count _____

One- Minute Read #2 Word Count _____

This is what I noticed about my fluency: _____

_____

_____

_____

_____

_____

_____

_____

_____

_____

_____

One-Minute Reading Word Count Record Sheet

Name _____

Book or Text Title _____

One- Minute Read #1 Word Count _____

One- Minute Read #2 Word Count _____

This is what I noticed about my fluency: _____

_____

_____

_____

_____

_____

_____

_____

_____

_____

Literacy Station: Fluency
Activity: Reader's Theater

Strategy Focus: Cooperative learning; Use correct prosody and intonation; Oral presentations

Materials: Cover, page 85; student directions, page 86; one two-pocket folder (one of each per script); one or more Reader's Theater scripts that your students may choose from for each station cycle (copies to supply all of your students with script choices); and a basket to store the script folders

From Sandy: I keep a separate file folder for each different script my students may use during the year. Include several copies of each script in the folder. Glue the directions to each folder. I then have the option of putting one script out at a time or giving them a choice of scripts. I sometimes choose to carry over social studies or science connections using themed scripts. I can also put out multiple scripts for variety and student choice. This can be powerful for students who may want to create a different interpretation on a previously used script. Let them release their inner creative selves as they build fluency!

Preparing the Station:

1. Glue the cover from page 85 to the front of a two-pocket folder. Glue the student directions from page 86 to the back of the folder. Laminate for durability.

2. Store multiple copies of each Reader's Theater script in each folder.

3. Set out only those you plan to use each cycle in the station basket.

Activity Introduction:

Review the differences between plays and reader's theater experiences with your students if you haven't done that yet. There are minimal, if any, props and costumes, in a reader's theater experience. Readers communicate the meaning in mood, emotion, and action by the clear expression and dialogue between the characters in the reading. Model with students as a performer yourself. Take on numerous roles, so they see the power of changing voices. Explain the student station directions and clarify any questions.

Differentiation for All Students:

1. Mix students heterogeneously for this activity. The strengths and weaknesses of all tend to be of great assets to one another in these readings. You may need to predetermine roles according to reading levels, but we find that with enough practice, most students can learn a script that motivates them.

2. Be sure that if you don't have mixed-ability groupings, your scripts are leveled appropriately for the students who will be reading them, be it struggling or advanced readers.

3. Challenge more confident readers to choose a common piece of text they have read and create their own scripts. This is a great way to demonstrate understanding. They can create book commercials for other readers.

Reader's Theater Script Title:

Reader's Theater

Directions

1. Choose a group of friends to read with for fluency practice during this station cycle.

2. Together, choose a script from the Reader's Theater script basket.

3. Read the entire script to yourself the first time.

4. You and your friends will need to select roles. If you are having trouble assigning people to specific parts, write the names of the characters on pieces of paper, fold them, and select randomly.(Remember: Anyone can read ANY role by changing his or her voice a bit!)

5. Practice this script in your roles during station time and be prepared to share it with the rest of the class at the end of the cycle.

Literacy Station: Fluency
Activity: Recording Studio

Strategy Focus: Demonstrate ability to read on grade level

Materials: Cover, page 88; student directions, page 89; Reflection Sheets, page 90 (copies for every student in your class); student-selected reading material (fiction or non-fiction); individual tape recorders; cassette tapes; headphones; one 10"x 13"envelope

NOTE: If your tape recorder is not electric, be sure to have up-to-date batteries in sufficient supply! Additionally, you may want to provide each student with one cassette tape to use repeatedly over the year. Write each student's name on their cassette with permanent marker, and store alphabetically in a covered shoebox. This will make a great end-of-year gift as well.

Preparing the Station:

1. Glue the cover from page 88 to the front of a large manila envelope. Glue the student directions from page 89 to the back of the manila envelope. Laminate for durability.

2. Store the Reflection Sheets in the envelope for student use in the station.

3. Have the tape recorder(s), blank tapes, and headphones set up in the station.

Activity Introduction:

1. If your students are not familiar with how to record using a cassette player, you will have to conduct a mini-lesson before introducing this station to them.

2. Once they know how to use the recorder, this can be powerful to build fluency—sometimes kids just have never heard themselves read. Model it for them so they can see you and HEAR you on the recorder.

3. Remind the students of the importance of selecting a passage they enjoy from their anchor text. Have them practice until they are comfortable with it.

4. Explain the student station directions and clarify any questions.

Differentiation for All Students:

1. Struggling readers may find support from reading with a buddy. The partners can assist one another and provide support in many ways.

2. Advanced readers may want to challenge themselves by setting goals for their reading. Perhaps they want to improve their expression in the second reading. Honing in on a particular aspect, other than"speed,"may help these readers greatly.

Recording Studio

Name _____ Date _____

Recording Studio

Directions:

Select a book to read. Think about using a portion of your anchor text from this cycle. It can be fiction or non-fiction.

1. Choose a favorite passage to read to yourself.

2. When you are ready, put a tape in the tape recorder and get ready to record yourself.

3. Now read it aloud into the tape recorder as you record yourself.

4. After you finish reading the passage, STOP the player. Push REWIND to bring the tape to the beginning and push PLAY to listen to yourself. (If there are headphones at the station, use them so you can really concentrate on only your voice.)

5. You are ready to record yourself reading the same passage again. Repeat steps 4 and 5.

6. Next, complete a Reflection Sheet to compare your two readings. Keep this in your Station Work Folder.

Name _____ Date _____

 # Recording Studio Reflection Sheet

What did you notice about your two readings?

First Reading:

_____
_____
_____
_____
_____
_____
_____
_____

Second Reading:

_____
_____
_____
_____
_____
_____
_____

How were they alike or different?

_____
_____
_____
_____
_____
_____

Chapter 8
Listening and Speaking

Listening and speaking may seem fairly straight-forward, but these are skills that deserve their own home in literacy stations. Listening skills are different than hearing. While students may hear what you are saying, or hear one another, how well do they really listen? When we talk about listening, we are referring to active, or attentive, listening. Students need to be able to have their eyes on the speaker, listen respectfully, and if appropriate for the situation, respond to what is being said.

Speakers, likewise, need to do more than just talk. Students need to pace their words, not too slow, not too fast, and they need to pronounce what they read clearly. Knowing what type of voice to use in any given situation is important. For instance, students need to know that during Buddy Reading, they should use a softer, almost whispering voice, and that it is appropriate to use a louder "stage voice" for presenting a Reader's Theater script.

Pages	Activity Name	Strategy Focus
92-95	Computer Presentation	Make an oral presentation using technology that is available
96-98	Karaoke	Give an oral presentation with appropriate eye contact, voice, and body movement
99-100	Merry-Go-Round Reading	Be an attentive listener and read with correct voice and pacing
101-112	Question Me	Listen to information presented orally to understand and make inferences
113-120	Research and Present It	Plan, organize, create, and give an oral presentation

Literacy Station: Listening & Speaking
Activity: Computer Presentation

Strategy Focus: Use voice, eye contact, and body movements to convey a message; Attend to an oral presentation and identify details from oral presentations

Materials: Student directions, fiction and informational-text computer presentation samples, pages 93-95; one colored manila folder; computers; individual student reading selections (fiction or non-fiction)

Preparing the Station:

1. Glue student directions to outside of the manila folder.

2. Glue the informational-text presentation to the inside left side of the folder.

Activity Introduction:

1. Explain how to create a computer presentation slideshow with your students. We suggest a very simple four to five slide format.

2. Once students understand how to create one, you can show them the activity materials and explain that they can use any book to complete this activity. They must be careful, however, to choose the correct sample slideshow for informational or fiction based on what type of book they are using.

3. Create one sample of each type of slideshow, just as the students will be doing, with either a class read-aloud book, the basal, or content text. This modeling is critical, especially with so many options available to students. Set very specific boundaries and other requirements, based upon your students' technological experience. You can leave these class-created samples as printed handouts in the station area for their reference.

4. Plan to set aside some special time for sharing these because so many students will be interested in seeing and hearing what their peers have to say.

Differentiation for All Students:

1. Struggling students will benefit from working in pairs or teams. The support they receive from one another, not only with the text but with the technological aspects of this activity, are huge.

2. More advanced students, or those who want to experience a bit of a challenge, can choose to add more slides to their presentations. They can expand the presentation by adding further visual and creative elements, such as sound effects, and animations as well.

Computer Presentation

1. Think about a book you have read and know well.

2. Plan and create a slideshow to share in class.

3. Make at least four slides.

4. If your book is fiction, your slides must include: characters, setting, problem, solution.

5. If your book is informational, then your slides must include four things you learned while reading.

6. Share your slideshow with the rest of the class.

The Three Bears

Characteristics:

The three bears:

Papa Bear
Mama Bear
Baby Bear

Goldilocks

Setting

- The three bears' house in the woods

Problem

- The bears' porridge was too hot.
- Goldilocks comes inside their house and eats their porridge, breaks their chairs, and sleeps in their beds.

Solution

- The bears come home and find Goldilocks sleeping in their beds. They scare her away and she is never seen near their house again.

Dolphins

Dolphins swim gracefully in the ocean. They breathe through a hole in the top of their head.

Manatees

Manatees are large ocean creatures but are quite gentle. They are sometimes injured by boat propellers as they swim in shallow waters.

Pelicans

Pelicans are birds that have a large pocket-shaped bill. They use it to scoop up water and smaller fish for their food.

Sea Turtles

Female sea turtles lay their eggs in deep nests in the sand. After several months, many tiny sea turtles hatch and try to make their way back into the ocean.

Literacy Station: Listening & Speaking
Activity: Karaoke

Strategy Focus: Oral presentations for a variety of purposes and audiences; Use context clues to determine meanings of unfamiliar words

Materials: Cover and student directions, pages 97-98; one 10" x 13" brown envelope; teacher-generated song list and laminated copies of song lyrics OR student copies of songs (see activity introduction for explanation); highlighters (for student copies) OR vis-à-vis markers (for laminated copies) of songs; tape player/CD player/karaoke machine; a microphone or two (even created, to use as props)

Preparing the Station:

1. Glue the cover to the front of the envelope and the student directions to the back.
2. Teacher Options: You will need to decide, based on the availability of your music materials, how you will set up this activity. You can have a list of songs for which you have recordings. Enlarge the lyrics, print them, and have them laminated. The students could then use the markers to mark their unknown words.
3. You could also have multiple copies of the song choices printed and housed in some way, perhaps in separate folders. With this system, they can use the highlighters. The choice is yours.
4. Set up a fun, creative area with the recording equipment you have available. While an actual karaoke machine is ideal and fun, this absolutely can be done with a tape or CD player. Give it a try and let your superstars shine!

Activity Introduction:

1. This is a fun and engaging activity. Most students enjoy singing along with the radio or television, and some may have karaoke machines of their own. Try some sing-a-long type songs with your class to get them familiarized with the karaoke concept if you have not done anything like this yet. Project the lyrics for all to view simultaneously, either with an interactive whiteboard, an overhead projector, or an enlarged chart.
2. Make sure you preview any lyrics you choose to use for appropriate content.

Differentiation for All Students:

1. Less confident students benefit from working together in teams or pairs. The assistance they give one another with vocabulary is significant, but it can also help with any insecurity they may have with public speaking.
2. Just as the struggling students may need teamwork for support, more confident students sometimes like the creativity they can come up with in groups. Let your students blossom with this experience and have a ball, all while learning! Imagine!

KARAOKE

Directions:

Choose a song from the music in the Listening and Speaking Station.

1. Read it at least three times.

2. Use a highlighter or marker to find any new or unknown words.

3. Discuss with a partner and use context clues to think of the meaning of these words.

4. Check in a dictionary to see if your guesses were correct.

5. Now practice reading the song at least three more times to make sure you understand its meaning.

6. Next, practice singing the song so you will be prepared for your performance!

7. Perform your song for someone else in the room. What a star!

Literacy Station: Listening & Speaking
Activity: Merry-Go-Round Reading

Strategy Focus: To be an attentive listener and read with correct voice and pacing

Materials: Student directions, page 100; one 9"x 12"piece of construction paper or vellum

Preparing the Station:

1. Glue the directions from page 100 to the construction paper or vellum. Laminate for durability.

2. Display in the station for students to view during station time.

Activity Introduction:

1. Explain that students can use any book they are currently reading to practice reading with a small group. This could be done with each student using the same text or they may each choose a different book.

2. Each student chooses a small amount of their text to read. When one reader stops the next one starts immediately reading his or her selection. This is such a fun station for students because it allows them to develop great oral reading skills while becoming strong listeners.

3. You can also develop a signal for the reader to give to show when he or she is done reading. They must listen carefully to the "signal" they agreed upon in order for the flow of the text to go smoothly.

4. Explain that if done correctly, it should sound like the rhythm of a merry-go-round!

5. Remind students that they should pay attention to any books that sound interesting during this activity. By listening to the other selections, students are exposed to other books they may want to select for future anchor text.

Differentiation for All Students:

1. Below-level readers may do well with starting this station as a partner activity. Often these students hesitate to read aloud. They may find a stronger sense of security in working with one other person initially. Once their confidence is bolstered, you can have them branch out to practice oral reading and listening skills with more than one student.

2. Advanced-level readers may want to be very creative with their signals for the turn taking. Instead of just a new page or new paragraph, they can change with specific character parts, or even have one child read as the narrator and the others take turns with the quoted dialogue lines in a fiction piece. Let them have fun with this!

Merry-Go-Round Reading

Directions:

1. Find three other people you would like to read with. You can all use the same book or choose different books. The books can be fiction or non-fiction.

2. Reread the book to find a favorite part. Make sure you choose a part that is not too long or too short.

3. Practice your reading selection.

4. Decide on some special way to signal each other that it is the next person's turn. (HINT: If you are using the same text, you may choose to read a paragraph or a page.)

5. Sit in a circle and read your selections one right after the other.

6. When each of you can read your part smoothly, it will sound like a merry-go-round!

Literacy Station: Listening & Speaking
Activity: Question Me

Strategy Focus: Listen to information presented orally to understand and make inferences about text

Materials: Student directions, answer flap, and questions cards, pages 102–112; construction paper or vellum; hole punch; one O-ring; one 10"x 13" brown envelope; pencils; and sticky notes

Preparing the Station:

1. Glue the directions from page 103 to the front of a large manila envelope. Tape the top of the answer flap from page 102 to the station back of the brown envelope. Laminate. You will need to slit the edges of the answer flap with a sharp tool so that it can be lifted up during the game.

2. Cut the question cards from pages 105-112. Fold and cut each piece of construction paper or vellum in half. Glue each card onto each of the eighteen pieces of paper. Laminate for durability. Then hole punch in the top corner and thread onto the O-ring to create your question card ring.

3. Put the question card ring inside the envelope.

Activity Introduction:

1. Explain that students can use any book they are currently reading to play this questioning game with a small group. They should, however, try to use their anchor text when appropriate. They must have books in common that they have all recently read.

2. This is such a fun station for students because it allows them to talk about their reading, yet actually play a game. Go ahead and make it fun when you can; it will get them hooked! The variety of questions allow for all types of literature to be included in the activity.

3. You may want to play a quick game of Twenty Questions with your students to show them the similarities to this station activity.

Differentiation for All Students:

1. Have lower-level readers choose common books or familiar readings to base their questions on from those they have done together, such as selections done in shared or guided reading groups. This can further reinforce concepts learned and review skills the questions address.

2. More confident readers can develop other neutral questions that could be added to the question list. If they come up with enough, have them create a second Twenty Questions card ring!

Question Me!
Answer Flap

Question Me!

1. Work with two or three other students.

2. Make a list of several books you all know and have read. Remember to include your anchor text when you can.

3. Choose one person to be "it."

4. "It" chooses one of the books from the list without telling anyone else. (Write the title on a sticky note and put it under the "answer flap.")

5. The rest of the group can ask "it" up to 20 "yes" or "no" questions about the book title. Use the question book to help you.

6. When someone thinks he or she knows the title, he or she can write it on a sticky note and look under the flap.

7. If the group guesses the title first, they win. If they do not guess (or give an incorrect guess), then "it" gets a point.

Group Learning Log

1. Who worked in your group today?
   _____
   _____

2. What books did you discuss?
   _____
   _____

3. How did the questioning help you figure out the titles?
   _____
   _____

Group Learning Log

1. Who worked in your group today?
   _____
   _____

2. What books did you discuss?
   _____
   _____

3. How did the questioning help you figure out the titles?
   _____
   _____

Group Learning Log

1. Who worked in your group today?
   _____
   _____

2. What books did you discuss?
   _____
   _____

3. How did the questioning help you figure out the titles?
   _____
   _____

Group Learning Log

1. Who worked in your group today?
   _____
   _____

2. What books did you discuss?
   _____
   _____

3. How did the questioning help you figure out the titles?
   _____
   _____

Question ideas for Question Me!

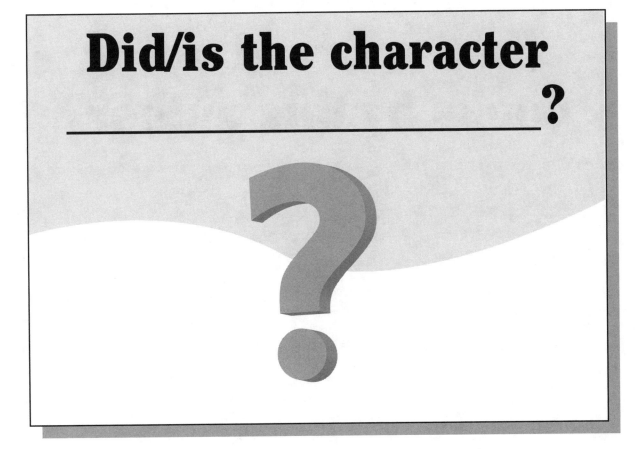

Did/is the character

_____ ?

Is this a chapter book?

Have we read other books by this author?

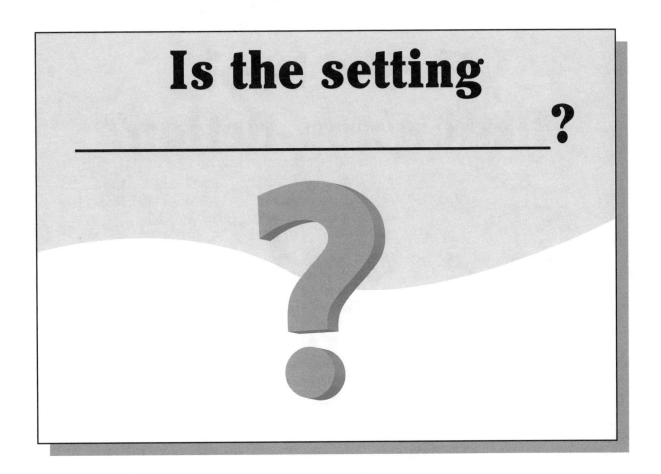

Is the setting _____?

Was there a problem/solution?

Is the book fiction/non-fiction?

Are there illustrations?

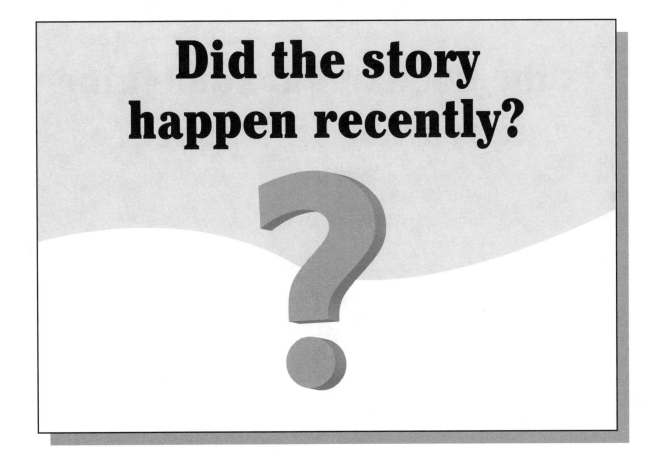

Is the story about the future?

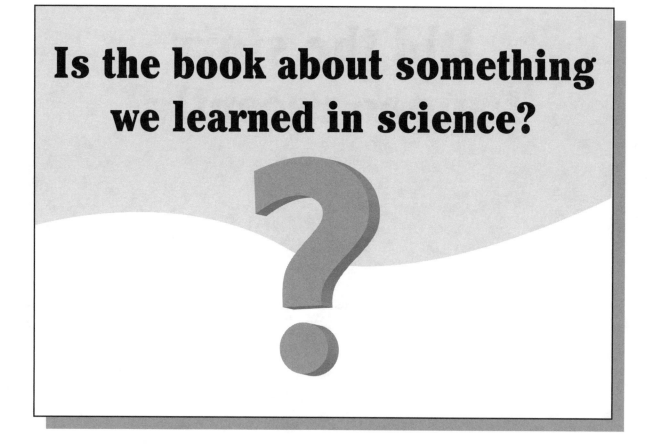

Is the book about something we learned in science?

Are there tables, graphs, or charts?

Is the book about something we learned in social studies?

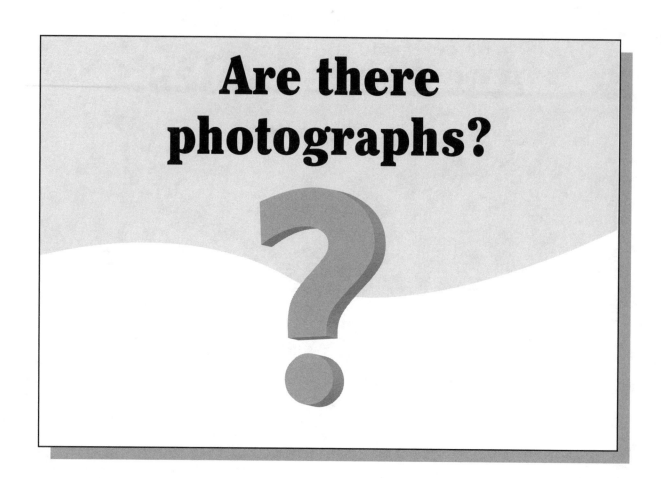

Are there photographs?

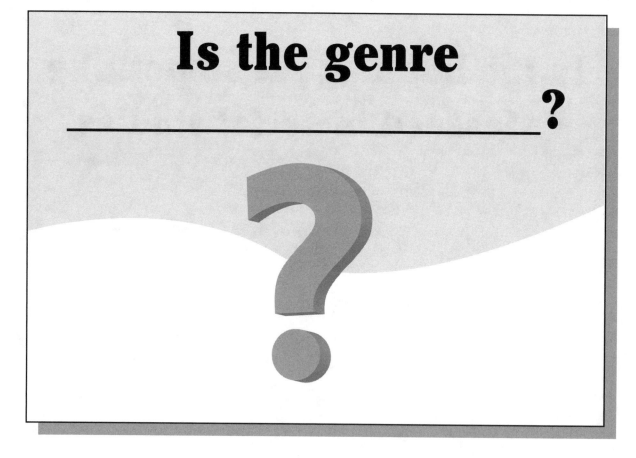

Is the genre

_____ ?

Literacy Station: Listening & Speaking
Activity: Research and Present It

Strategy Focus: Plan, organize, create, and give an oral presentation

Materials: Student directions, Presentation Ideas sheet, Planning for Research and My Research Evaluation sheets (enough copies for all students); pocket labels/sign-up sheet, pages 115-120; one colored two-pocket folder; one 9"x 12" piece of construction paper; a vis-à-vis marker; pencils; highlighters; index cards; notebook paper; and, based on your students' abilities, research/reference materials and Internet access

Preparing the Station:

1. Glue the directions from page 115 to the front of a colored two-pocket folder. Glue the Presentation Ideas from page 118 to the back of the folder. Glue the pocket labels to each side of the inside pockets. Laminate both the folder and the sign-up sheet.

2. Slit the pockets open to store the student research plan and evaluation sheets.

3. Hang the sign-up sheet near the station and have a vis-à-vis marker available for students to sign up when they are ready to share their presentation with the class.

Activity Introduction:

Before adding this activity, instruct students in how to conduct research about a specific topic using various resources from reference books, non-fiction text, or the Internet. Explain that researchers must be able to record little "nuggets" of information rather than entire sentences, then to transfer that information into complete sentences when they write about it in their final product.

1. Explain that they can research any topic they want to learn more about.

2. The power in this station is that it not only covers Listening and Speaking, as we have it categorized, but also comprehension of the material they are reading. Additionally, they are able to choose how they want to present it. There are some awesome opportunities for higher-level thinking skills in this station. Teach it once, keep it all year!

Differentiation for All Students:

1. Lower-level readers may benefit from working with a partner or giving a small group presentation as a team.

2. More confident students should truly take off with this one. Allow them the flexibility to embellish and add to any presentation to show what information they gained from their research.

3. This is another station that may extend beyond the two-week cycle. This should be encouraged as it is often a sign of deep learning and engagement.

Research **IT!**

1. Choose something that you want to learn more about. Write out two to four key questions that you would like to have answered in your research.

2. Use the materials and resources in our room or in the Media Center to read and find out more about your topic.

3. Decide how you will collect information. Will you need note cards? Will you make copies? Will you need to print out information from a computer?

4. Use a highlighter or sticky notes to mark the parts of information you will use to make your presentation.

5. Plan your presentation. (See the idea list on the other side of this folder.)

6. Sign up for a day or time to present your work.

7. Fill out your evaluation.

1,2, 3...

Planning for Research

Name: _____ Date: _____

Key Questions (You must have two to four):

1. _____

2. _____

3. _____

4. _____

Materials and Resources I Used:

_____ _____ _____

_____ _____ _____

_____ _____ _____

_____ _____ _____

Here's how I will present my information: _____

_____

_____

_____

Materials I will need: _____

_____

_____

_____

I will present my project on: _____

**Don't forget to fill out your evaluation when you are finished!

My Research Evaluation

Name: _____   Date: _____

Write your key questions here. Remember that you must have two to four. Check the box next to each question if you were able to answer it from your research and in your presentation.

☐ 1. _____
☐ 2. _____
☐ 3. _____
☐ 4. _____

Are there questions you did not get answered? _____
Why or why not? _____

How did your method of information collection help you?
_____

What surprised you about your research? _____
_____

What do you think you did really well? _____
_____

What do you think you could have done differently?
_____

What did you like most about doing this project? _____
_____

What would you like to research next? _____
_____

Presentation Ideas

PowerPoint presentation

Write a poem or song

Create a tri-fold display

Make a reader's theater play

Create a small book

Make an informational quilt

Write a speech

Create a brochure

Make a model

Make a poster

Write a report

Your own idea (must get teacher approval)

Planning for Research

My Research Evaluations

Sign-in Sheet for Presentations

Are you ready to present?

Write your name, topic, and format to reserve a time to share with the class.

Name	Presentation Topic and Format

Chapter 9:
Visual Literacy

Visual literacy is the ability to interpret and make meaning from information presented as images in our world. It is directly tied to what we see and our perception of it. As our culture continues to change, visual literacy is vital to our everyday lives. Visual texts are those that convey meaning through a combination of images, patterns, charts, diagrams, and text. Text is not always present.

Artistic representations are key to developing this type of literacy. In many schools, creative visual responses to literature and learning have been replaced by testing and workbook practice. We believe it must be brought back to the classroom as a way of helping students express their thinking and demonstrate their understanding of reading and the world around them. It is our hope that your students will discover some of that creativity and fun, while learning and fostering visual literacy skills in this station.

Pages	Activity Name	Strategy Focus
122-125	Create a Model	Organize information to show important details in charts, graphs, and other visual representations
126-130	Create a Scene	Create a two- or three-dimensional representation of literature
131-133	Food for Thought	Respond to environmental print in order to find details
134-137	Vocabulary Chains	Connect and categorize vocabulary, then display it in a creative way
138-140	Vocabulary Word Art	Develop visual representations of key vocabulary words learned in class

Literacy Station: Visual Literacy
Activity: Create a Model

Strategy Focus: Organize information to show important details in charts, graphs, and other visual representations

Materials: Station pages 123-125 (cover, student directions, and response sheet—enough for your whole class); construction paper, in various colors; markers/colored pencils; student-selected non-fiction books; and a 10"x 13" manila envelope

Preparing the Station:

1. Glue the cover, page 123, to the front of the brown envelope. Glue the student directions, page 124, to the back of the envelope. Laminate for durability.

2. Be sure to have construction paper and other art materials available in the station for student use.

3. Put copies of Response Sheet, page 125, in the brown envelope.

Activity Introduction:

1. This activity helps students express their understanding of informational text with the use of a visual aid. It could be a graphic organizer, table, chart, or graph. The limits are only based on what you have modeled in your classroom. Create a classroom chart with some of the visual presentations they have seen in books such as various types of graphs, charts, and diagrams. As students discover more, let them add a sample to the poster. This will keep the station fresh for quite some time!

2. Explain the station directions to students and clarify any questions they have.

Differentiation for All Students:

1. Students who are struggling with comprehension of informational text will benefit from working with another student. Having another person to help provide support while finding key information in the text, as well as show how to display that information clearly on a chart or other visual display, can be a great asset to these students.

2. More confident readers can be asked to display their information in two or more ways or to compare and contrast several bits of information.

3. Remind students that this is a great activity to choose when their anchor text is informational.

Create a Model

Create a Model

Directions:

1. Choose a non-fiction book that you find interesting and want to learn more about.

2. Use the Table of Contents to pick the sections that are the most interesting to you. Read carefully to find new information about this topic.

3. Get a Response Sheet from the station envelope. Think of what new information you learned. Write these facts down on the response sheet.

4. Consider ways you could visually display this information for others to read. Brainstorm a list of different charts, graphs, or graphic organizers you could create in the box on the response sheet.

5. Circle your favorite and then use the materials in the station to make it.

6. Display your finished product in the room for your classmates to view. Be sure your name and the title of the book are on it.

Name_____ Date_____

Create a Model

Response Sheet

Book title:

_____

The topic that interests me: _____

After reading from this book, what new information did you
learn about this topic? _____
_____

Brainstorm ways that you could visually display this information.
When you have made a list, circle your favorite one and go
create it!

_____

_____

_____

_____

_____

How will your model help others understand this topic?

_____

_____

_____

_____

_____

_____

Literacy Station: Visual Literacy
Activity: Create a Scene

Materials: Station pages 128-130 (cover, student directions, and response sheet—enough for your whole class); construction paper, in various colors; other art materials as available; scissors; glue sticks; markers/colored pencils; and a 10" x 13" brown envelope

> **From Sandy:** I have assorted "collage" materials that can be collected easily by having students and families bring in buttons, fabric, yarn, wrapping paper, and ribbon remnants from home. To this we can add recyclables, such as clean popsicle sticks, bits of aluminum foil, and random sizes of cardboard, foam trays, and egg cartons. It will be a great start to your "collage box." Enjoy collecting!

Preparing the Station:

1. Glue the cover, page 128, to the front of the brown envelope. Glue the student directions, page 129, to the back of the envelope. Laminate for durability.

2. Keep construction paper and the other art materials available in the station for student use.

3. Put copies of the Response Sheet, page 130, in the brown envelope.

Activity Introduction:

1. This station activity allows students to express themselves artistically and creatively while responding to a favorite scene from a book. Make sure you have explained the story element of setting before introducing this activity.

2. Remind students that they can use their anchor text for this activity if it is a fiction book. If it is an informational text, they still may be able to share a "scene" from it. Or they may want to recreate a scene from a whole class story.

3. A comparison of the 2-D and 3-D math concepts should be taught or reviewed for clarification as well.

4. Explain the station directions to students and clarify any questions they may have.

Differentiation for All Students:

1. Students who are struggling readers benefit from this activity because it requires little text negotiation. They may have the choice to orally share their scene creations with a partner or small group instead of writing about it. They can also tell someone else about their creation and then write with a partner about it.

2. Ask students who need more of a challenge to create a multiple-scene storyboard for their book and write about the scenes they selected. You may want to talk about the term "storyboarding" with them and have them investigate how this technique is often used to plan and prepare various forms of entertainment.

Create a Scene

Directions:

1. Select a key scene from a book you are currently reading.

2. Think about what you see in your mind's eye. Then decide how you would like to show this scene to others.

3. Use the art materials in the station to create either a 2-D or 3-D representation of your scene. Have fun and be creative!

4. Fill out a Response Sheet and write a descriptive paragraph explaining why you chose this scene from your book. Keep it in your Station Work Folder.

Name_____ Date_____

Create a Scene

Response Sheet

Book Title: _____

What scene did you choose for your visual representation?

_____
_____
_____
_____
_____
_____
_____

Explain why you picked this particular scene in your book.

_____
_____
_____
_____
_____
_____
_____

Literacy Station: Visual Literacy
Activity: Food For Thought

Strategy Focus: Respond to environmental print to find details

Materials: Empty food packages; station pages 132-133; colored manila folder; notebook paper; and pencils

Preparing the Station:

1. Collect several food boxes and packages. Prepare your food packages in one of several ways: You can collapse the boxes; some teachers prefer to cut them apart. Laminate them, and use a binding machine to secure the fronts and backs together. It depends on your preference and your storage capacity.

2. Glue the cover, page 132, to the front of the colored folder. Glue the student directions to the inside of the folder. Laminate for durability.

3. Be sure to have paper and pencils available in the station for student use.

Activity Introduction:

1. This station is a great way for students to practice using informational text. You should model this with your students initially using key words from the student directions to aid with understanding.

2. Explain the station directions to students and clarify any questions they may have.

3. As time passes, change the packages you include in the station to freshen up the activity.

Differentiation for All Students:

1. Have students bring in food boxes from their homes. This can lead to many great conversations. Based on your population, cultural eating differences may possibly be discovered, too (great for ESL students).

2. Students who work at a lower reading level may find it helpful to work with a partner to read and search for information in this activity.

3. Students who are ready for more of a challenge can take it a step further and create commercials for these products. They can then perform them for others, further developing their speaking and listening skills.

Food For Thought

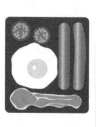    

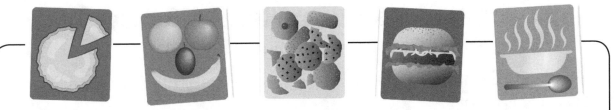

Food For Thought

1. Choose a food container or label.

2. Answer five questions in complete sentences on a piece of notebook paper. Be sure to write the number of the question you are answering by each sentence.

3. Put your finished work in your Station Work Folder.

QUESTIONS:

1. What shapes can you find?

2. How many vitamins and minerals are in this product?

3. How many descriptive words can you find?

4. How much does this package weigh?

5. How many servings are there in this package?

6. What is the fat content per serving?

7. How do you prepare this food?

8. How could you prepare a variation of this product?

Literacy Station: Visual Literacy
Activity: Vocabulary Chains

Strategy Focus: Create a colorful means to display vocabulary, connected and categorized in various ways

Materials: Cover, page 135; student directions, page 136; student-selected text (fiction or non-fiction); 9"x 12" construction paper; markers; tape, stapler, or glue sticks

Preparing the Station:

1. Cut enough paper strips from construction paper to have eight to ten per student. (Note: Make three folds lengthwise to end up with eight strips per page. It works out to be a good size for students to write on and to connect.)

2. Glue the cover from page 135 to the front of a large manila envelope. Glue the student directions from page 136 to the back of the manila envelope. Laminate for durability.

3. Put the Vocabulary Chain Reflection Sheets (page 137) and the paper strips in the brown envelope.

4. Keep markers, tape, staplers, or glue sticks in the station for student use.

Activity Introduction:

1. Students need to be able to relate to words in many different ways. There is great power in seeing how different people connect vocabulary words and can share their thinking.

2. Model this activity with your students using a familiar passage, such as a section of a read aloud book. Show how you connect several meaningful vocabulary words from it. Then have other students see if they can connect those same words in any other way and explain why they did so.

3. Model how to complete the Vocabulary Chain Reflection Sheet as well.

4. Remind students that they should use their anchor text for this activity.

5. Explain the student station directions and clarify any questions.

Differentiation for All Students:

1. Students who struggle with words and their meaning can search for fewer than the suggested eight to ten words. A smaller goal may help ensure success. Use personal judgment based on your individual students' needs and abilities.

2. Students who have difficulty connecting their chains right away may want to use sticky notes with the word written on them to plan their connections.

3. Above-level readers who are ready for a challenge may enjoy creating some additional variation of this on the opposite side of their strips before connecting them. They may write a sentence that includes the word, so the word's meaning is clear, or they could write a riddle whose answer is the vocabulary word.

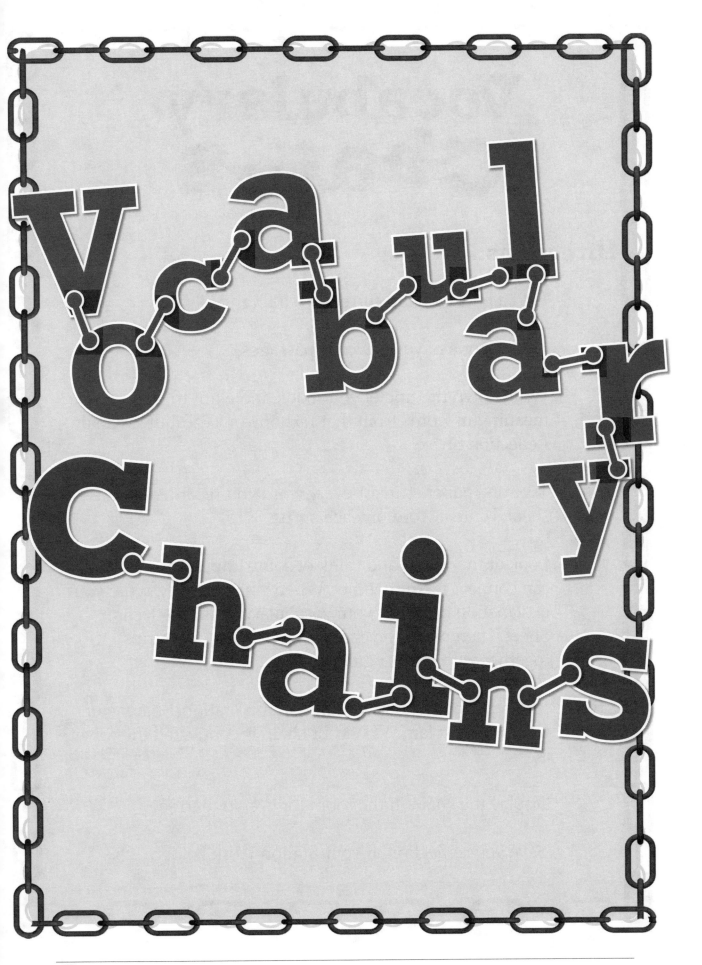

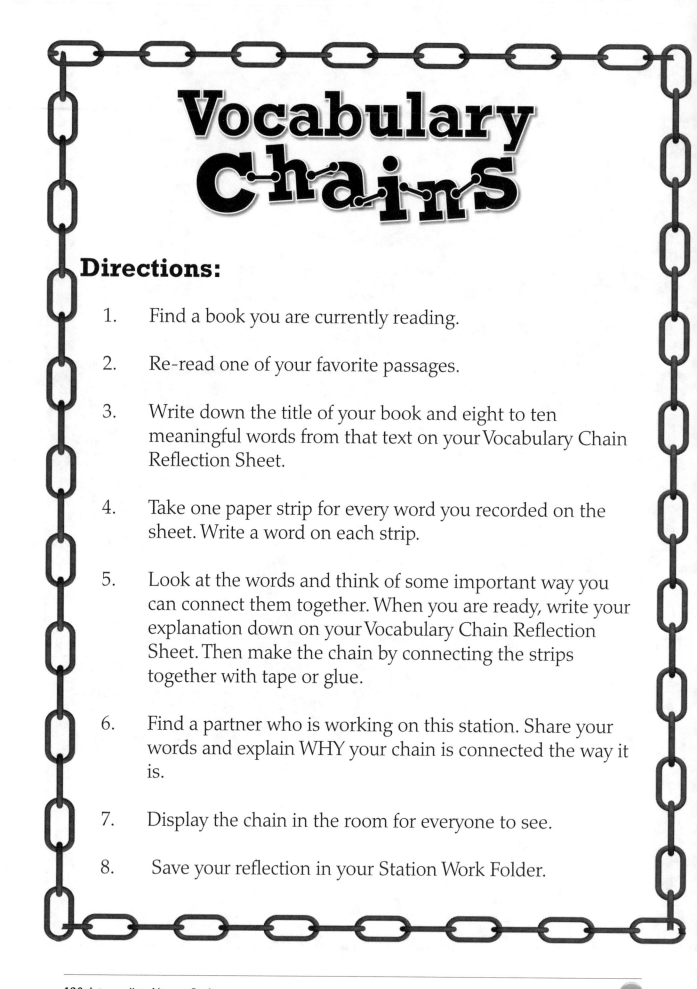

Vocabulary Chains

Directions:

1. Find a book you are currently reading.

2. Re-read one of your favorite passages.

3. Write down the title of your book and eight to ten meaningful words from that text on your Vocabulary Chain Reflection Sheet.

4. Take one paper strip for every word you recorded on the sheet. Write a word on each strip.

5. Look at the words and think of some important way you can connect them together. When you are ready, write your explanation down on your Vocabulary Chain Reflection Sheet. Then make the chain by connecting the strips together with tape or glue.

6. Find a partner who is working on this station. Share your words and explain WHY your chain is connected the way it is.

7. Display the chain in the room for everyone to see.

8. Save your reflection in your Station Work Folder.

Name_____ Date_____

Vocabulary Chains
Reflection Sheet

Book Title _____

Write eight to ten words that you found meaningful from the rereading of a passage in this book.

1.	6.
2.	7.
3.	8.
4.	9.
5.	10.

Think about how you can connect your words. Write them in some important order. Explain WHY you did it that way. Then share with a partner!

_____

_____

_____

_____

_____

_____

_____

Literacy Station: Visual Literacy
Activity: Vocabulary Word Art

Strategy Focus: Develop visual representations of key vocabulary words taught directly

Materials: 9" x 12" construction paper, in various colors; station pages, 139-140; brown envelope; scissors; glue sticks; markers/colored pencils; paints; any other desired art medium as available

Preparing the Station:

1. Glue the cover, page 139, to the front of the brown envelope. Glue the student directions, page 140, to the back of the envelope. Laminate for durability.

2. Be sure to have construction paper and the other art materials available in the station for student use.

3. Create a folder labeled "This Week's Vocabulary Words." In this, put each week's vocabulary words for students to check their spellings of the words they visualize before they create their posters.

Activity Introduction:

1. This station is a fun and creative way for students to practice using vocabulary words. The concept of visualization should have been previously taught to your students before putting this station out.

2. Explain the station directions to students and clarify any questions they may have.

Differentiation for All Students:

1. You can vary this to go along with any topic or any content area.

Note from Sandy: My students have practiced using their science vocabulary words by making posters in this station. They love getting creative and I love seeing them reinforce content area vocabulary in any way I can!

2. Struggling students may need the support of a vocabulary word list. Rather than just using the word list folder to check their words' spellings, they may need it for support as they think of the words initially.

3. Students who are more confident may want to challenge themselves to come up with synonyms and/or antonyms for any words that they can. Another option is having them include word meanings with the words they include on their posters.

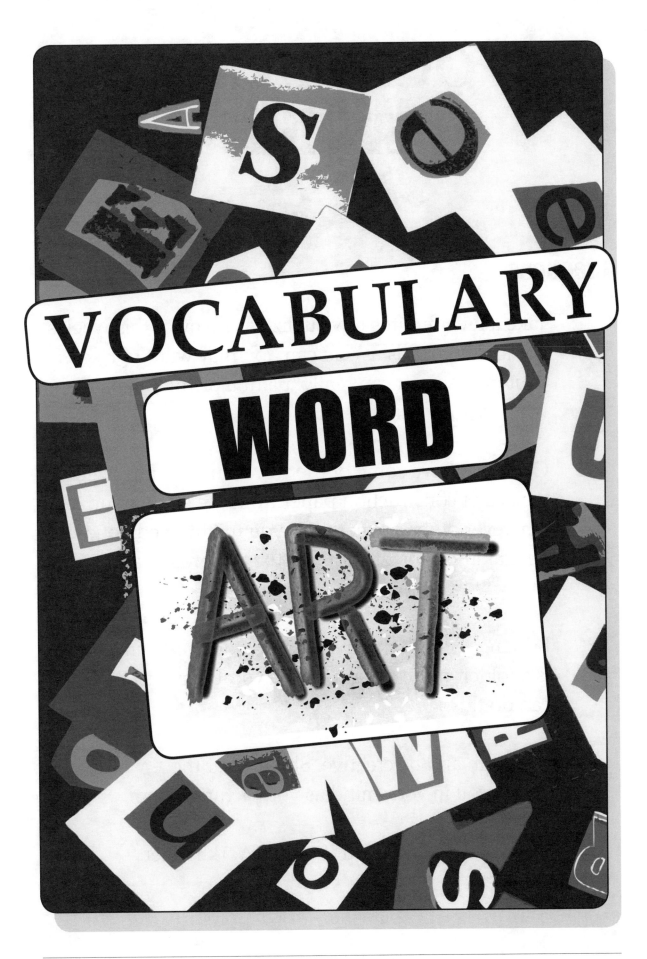

VOCABULARY

WORD

ART

VOCABULARY
WORD

Directions:

1. Take a few minutes to visualize as many of this week's vocabulary words as you can. You may want to close your eyes so you can really "paint a picture" of each word in your mind.

2. Once you have some of the words in your mind, get a piece of construction paper from the station and whatever other art materials you might need. You will be making a poster showing these words in any way that you want to.

3. Be sure to check the spelling of your words first. (There is a folder in the station with a vocabulary list so you can do this.)

4. Have fun and be creative. Show what these words look like to you in your mind as you pictured them!

5. Keep your work in your Station Work Folder.

Chapter 10
Word Work

Word Work is just that—working with words in many ways. We want your students to become familiar with vocabulary from the text they are reading and to go deeper with it. Sometimes you want them to think critically about ways words can be connected and categorized. Other times, you need to them to focus on word meanings and origins. You may want them to experience turning individual vocabulary words into sentences or even poems of their own. We want students to explore words in a multitude of ways to develop deeper, richer vocabularies. It will broaden their reading and writing abilities. Take a glimpse of the new ways you and your students can make words in this station.

Pages	Activity Name	Strategy Focus
142-143	Grab a Word, Make a Sentence	Use new vocabulary that is directly taught
144-145	Making Words	Creating words; Using dictionaries to confirm the meaning of new vocabulary words
146-149	Poetry Place	Identify and explain how language choice helps to develop mood and meaning in poetry; Use context clues to determine meaning of unknown words
150-155	Prefix/Suffix Word Play	Use meaning of familiar base word and affixes to create and determine the meaning of new words
156-158	Word Gathering	Categorize key vocabulary

Literacy Station: Word Work
Activity: Grab a Word, Make a Sentence

Strategy Focus: Demonstrate understanding of new vocabulary words by creating sentences

Materials: 3" x 5" cards with familiar vocabulary words printed on them; pens; pencil; dictionary; thesaurus

Preparing the Station:

1. Copy the directions from page 143 on a piece of vellum or cardstock. Adhere directions to the outside of a file folder or manila envelope.

2. Write one familiar vocabulary word on each index card and place inside the envelope.

3. Include a basket of the following supplies: paper, pencils, pens, dictionary, thesaurus.

Activity Introduction:

1. Once students have learned several vocabulary words, they are ready to begin this activity.

2. Explain to students that one way to learn new words is to use them in new sentences that are meaningful to them.

3. Choose an interesting word and have as many students as possible give a sentence using that word. Talk about the similarities and differences in students' sentences.

4. Read the student directions aloud as you model the process for students.

5. Let them practice reading all the vocabulary words inside the envelope. Explain that occasionally you will add brand new words to the envelope and remove others. Remind them that most of the time the words will come from your whole group instruction. Sometimes, however, you may want to ask students to add a word or two from their own anchor text.

6. After they have had practice, explain that they will be able to practice writing sentences using new vocabulary words when they complete this activity.

Differentiation for All Students:

1. For students who need additional support, provide word cards with a student friendly definition or picture on it.

2. Students who need more challenge may want to try using more than one word in the sentence.

3. You may also want to differentiate how many sentences you ask students to produce.

4. Have an anchor text week where each student picks three words from his or her book to put in the envelope.

Grab a Word, Make a Sentence

disaster **roam** **meander**

1. Choose five or more words from the word cards.

2. Make sure you know what each word means.

3. Write a sentence for each word you choose.

4. Share your sentences with someone else.

My mom said, "Your room is a disaster!"

Literacy Station: Word Work
Activity: Making Words

Strategy Focus: Create little words from big words; Use dictionaries to confirm meaning of new words

Materials: Directions, page 145; grid graph paper; index cards; 9"x 12" envelope or file folder; dictionary; paper; pencils

Preparing the Station:

1. Copy and laminate the directions from page 145.

2. Attach the directions to the front of a folder or envelope. Place graph paper and index cards inside the folder or envelope.

Activity Introduction:

1. Tell students that one way to learn more about words is to look for patterns in them. This activity will help them play with words and word patterns.

2. Read the directions aloud and discuss how to locate an interesting word. Remind students that the word they select should have at least six letters in it.

3. Model this process for students. Have them practice making small words with the word that you select.

4. Let them practice the activity with partners while you coach and model the procedures.

5. Remind students that looking for patterns in words and manipulating letters helps them know and understand words better.

Differentiation for All Students:

1. Students who need additional support can select a word with fewer than six letters. They can also work with a partner.

2. You may want to pre-designate the big word and allow students to make smaller words from it.

3. Have students choose several "big words" and see if their friends can guess all the words they chose.

MAKING WORDS

1. Select a word of six or more letters from a book you are reading.

2. Look up the word in the dictionary. Write it on an index card along with the definition.

3. Get a piece of graph paper and write each letter from the word in a grid square. Cut out the letter squares.

4. Arrange the letters to make little words.

5. Record each little word you can make from the big word on a piece of paper. Try to make at least ten words.

6. Give someone else your letter squares and see how many of your words he or she makes. Ask him or her to use all the letters to find your "big word."

7. Staple your definition card to the paper, and place your paper in the completed work folder.

Literacy Station: Word Work
Activity: Poetry Place

Strategy Focus: Identify and explain how language choice helps to develop mood and meaning in poetry; Use context clues to determine meaning of unknown words

Materials: Copies of appropriate poems; bulletin board paper or large chart paper; copies of the forms, pages 147-149; sticky notes; pens/pencils

Preparing the Station:

1. Fold a large piece of chart paper or bulletin board paper in four sections.
2. Copy and laminate the forms on pages 147–149.
3. Glue the forms from pages 147 and 148 to the top two sections.
4. Cut the headers on page 149 in half and adhere to the bottom two sections.
5. Place sticky notes and writing utensils near the station.

Activity Introduction:

1. Explain that reading poetry is sometimes like reading a short story. Good readers think about what it makes them think, feel, or remember.
2. Tell students that sometimes they will locate words or ideas that are new or unclear to them.
3. Have students write these words or ideas on small sticky notes and place them on the "I Need to Know" section of the chart.
4. Students should also add something they would like to ask or tell the poet. They can place this in the appropriate part of the chart.
5. Remind students they should also read other student's responses. This helps readers learn new thoughts and ideas.

Differentiation for All Students:

1. Match poems to your students' reading levels. Color code your reading groups and copy poems to the assigned group color. Students can read and respond to the poem that is at their reading level.
2. For students who need an additional challenge or extension, have them select their own poems to add to this station throughout the year.

Poetry Place

1. Read this week's poem.

2. Think about what the poem makes you think, feel, or remember.

3. Are there any words or ideas that confuse you?

4. Write these on the "I need to know" board.

5. What would you like to ask or tell the poet about the poem?

6. Write your thinking on the response chart.

Literacy Station: Word Work
Activity: Prefix/Suffix Word Play

Strategy Focus: Use meaning of familiar base words and affixes to create and determine the meaning of new words

Materials: Directions, page 151; response form, page 155; cardstock; file folders or manila envelope; index cards; small sandwich bag or envelope

Preparing the Station:

1. Copy the directions from page 151 on a piece of vellum or cardstock. Adhere them to the outside of a file folder or manila envelope.

2. Copy and cut out the prefix and suffix cards (pages 152-154). Duplicate the prefix cards on pink and the suffix cards on blue. Cut apart and place them in a small sandwich bag or envelope. If you use a file folder, adhere the envelope or bag to the inside cover.

3. Include a basket of the following supplies: pink and blue highlighters, small sticky notes, correction tape or correction fluid, dictionary and thesaurus.

Activity Introduction:

1. Once students are familiar with prefixes and suffixes, you can have them complete this activity.

2. Explain to students that parts of words often give us clues to meaning.

3. Use a familiar word such as "happy" to practice adding prefixes and/or suffixes to change its meaning.

4. Read the student directions aloud as you model the process for students.

5. Let them use the prefix or suffix cards to create new words.

6. After they have had practice, explain that they will be able to practice using words from books they read.

Differentiation for All Students:

1. For students who need additional support, provide word cards with the prefix or suffix already highlighted.

2. Students who need more challenge may want to try adding both a prefix and a suffix to a word.

Prefix and Suffix Word Play

1. Sort out the prefix and suffix cards.

2. (Hint: Prefixes are pink and suffixes are blue.)

3. Look for at least five words in your book that have prefixes or suffixes. Write each one on the response form.

4. Highlight prefixes in pink and suffixes in blue.

5. Try to create a new word by changing either the prefix or suffix. Write a definition for each new word.

6. Use these words in a sentence.

7. Be sure your name is on your paper.

8. Put your completed work away.

Prefix	A prefix is added to the beginning of a word.
anti-	opposing/ against/ the opposite of
dis-	to remove/to negate
in-	not/without OR in/into/inside/ towards
mis-	wrong/wrongly
pre-	before in time/ place/ order
re-	again
un-	not/reverse/ cancel
under-	beneath/below/ not enough

Suffix	A suffix is added to the end of a word.
-able	can be done
-er	"someone who" OR person connected with
-ful	full of
-less	without
-ly	characteristic of
-ment	action or process
-ness	state or condition of

___understand	pain___
___able	care___
___happy	report___
___play	paint___
___tie	use___
___write	teach___
___fill	favor___
___judge	understand___
___button	fear___
___spell	happ(y)___
___do	sad___
___assemble	empt(y)___

Name: _____ Date: _____

Prefix and Suffix Word Play

1. List at least five words from your book that have a prefix or a suffix:

1. _____ 2. _____ 3. _____

4. _____ 5. _____ 6. _____

7. _____ 8. _____ 9. _____

2. Highlight the prefixes in pink and the suffixes in blue.

3. Try to create a new word by changing either the prefix or the suffix.

4. Write a definition for each new word and use it in a sentence.

My word	I think it means…	My sentence

Literacy Station: Word Work
Activity: Word Gathering

Strategy Focus: Categorizing key vocabulary

Materials: Sorting mats made from bulletin board paper; sticky notes; student response form, page 158; 9"x 12" manila envelope

Preparing the Station:

1. Copy and laminate the directions from page 157.

2. Create two sorting mats using bulletin board paper or large pieces of construction paper. Fold these mats into four sections.

3. Make several copies of the student response form on page 158 and place them in the envelope.

Activity Introduction:

1. Explain to students that they will practice working with words in this station. Begin by discussing where interesting words can be found in the classroom. This might include books you are reading both in groups and independently, wall charts, writing folders, poetry, etc.

2. Have students help you gather ten to twenty words from their environment.

3. Read the directions aloud and model for students how to create a word sort using the mat.

4. Discuss other ways the words could be sorted.

5. Tell students they will follow this same procedure with this activity using words they select individually.

Differentiation for All Students:

1. Students who need additional support can select fewer words and work with a partner or small group to create a word sort.

2. Have students who need an additional challenge create more than one sort for their selected words. Help them understand that sorting and categorizing words is a higher-order thinking skill.

Word Gathering

1. Look around our room for some words you like.

2. Choose 10 to 20 words.

3. Write each word on a sticky note or index card.

4. Sort your words on the sorting mat.

5. When you sort, think about letter sounds, syllables, word meanings, etc.

6. Show your sort to someone else.

7. See if he or she can guess your sort.

8. Fill out the sorting form and place it in the "finished work" basket.

Word Gathering

Name: _____ Date: _____

My Word Sort (Use at least two boxes):

Write about your sort.

1. Label each section to tell what the words have in common.

2. Why did you choose to sort these words this way?

3. How did thinking about these words help you understand them or know them better?

Chapter 11
Written Response

In many cases, teachers ask students to read a passage then share some bit of information about it. Often this is in a discussion format. But, assessment situations require students to be able to respond in writing to what they have read independently. They may have had little exposure to this type of reading followed by written response. That hardly seems fair, does it? We believe they need regular practice reading with a written response to a variety of text. Students need to be able to clearly explain what they are being asked to discuss and respond accordingly. These activities provide an assortment of written responses to both fiction and informational text. Some enable you to concentrate on very specific writing skills and others are more open-ended. All of them will help your students hone their skills at communicating a message through writing.

Pages	Activity Name	Strategy Focus
160-164	Create-a-Story Matrix	Identify characters, setting, and problem; Brainstorm ideas; Narrative writing
165-168	Digging Deeper	Informational text research and written response; Compare text for further details
169-176	My Reading Journal	Write in various formats; Respond to specific questions based on fiction or non-fiction text
177-180	Nose for News	News article writing; Respond to specific headlines and topic questions
180-183	What a Character!	Character trait descriptions based on reading; Give support and evidence in writing

Literacy Station: Written Response
Activity: Create-a-Story Matrix

Strategy Focus: Identify characters, setting and problem; Brainstorm ideas; Narrative writing

Materials: Chart labels, cover sheet, and student directions, pages 162-164; 18"x 24"piece of construction paper (or bulletin board paper); packs of sticky notes; pencils/markers; one colored file folder; students'independent reading books and writing journals

Preparing the Station:

1. Create a matrix mat by dividing the 18"x 24"piece of construction paper into four lengthwise columns, each 4 ½"x 24".

2. Use chart labels from page 164 to label the top of columns with the following headings in this order: Good Characters, Bad Characters, Setting, and Problem. Laminate before using in the station.

3. Glue the cover, page 162, to the front of the brown envelope, and glue the student directions, page 163, to the back of the envelope. Laminate for durability.

4. Display the poster on a wall in the station so students can easily reach the chart.

5. Have the directions, sticky notes, and writing instruments available nearby.

Activity Introduction:

1. In shared reading lessons, you should have discussed how some characters can be "good"or more positive, while others have qualities that demonstrate that they are more negative in their nature. We will call these the"bad"characters. This will be a building block to instruction in later years about protagonists and antagonists in literature. Additionally, students must be aware of the ideas of setting and problem of stories in order to successfully manage this station independently.

2. Read the station directions to them, explaining any questions that arise.

3. Model the station procedures, using the sticky notes to put the names of good and bad characters, settings, and problems from favorite class books.

4. Teachers should randomly remove several sticky notes from each column at least once each ten-day cycle. This will keep the matrix fresh with new ideas and keep this station going indefinitely.

Differentiation for All Students:

1. For struggling students, limiting the size of paper to a half sheet can give them a sense that the task is not so overwhelming to complete. Partners may also work on a shared writing story, feeding off each other's strengths.

2. For more advanced students, you may want to encourage them to write an ongoing story, developing their characters in a chapter-by-chapter format. They may want to add a new character, setting, or problem from time to time.

3. Students may also maintain their own personal matrix in their writing journals to use for independent writing time.

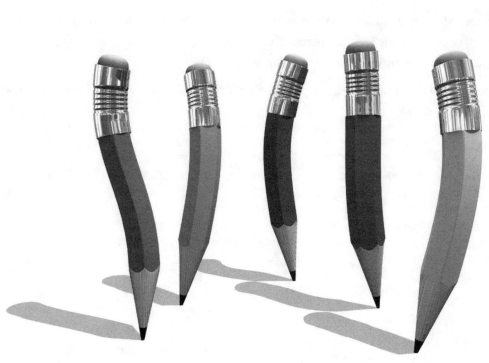

Create
-a-
Story Matrix

Create-a-Story Matrix

1.   Use your anchor text or another book you have read. Select the name of any good or bad character, a setting, or a problem that a character faced in the book.

2.   Write that on one of the sticky notes provided in the station and add it to the matrix mat under the correct column heading.

3.   Now choose one good character, one bad character, one setting, and one problem. Write these four ideas in your journal on a new page.

4.   Now start to brainstorm! Develop a story using all four of these elements. Be creative!

5.   Put your paper in your Station Work Folder.

Chart Labels

Good Characters

Bad Characters

Setting

Problem

Literacy Station: Written Response
Activity: Digging Deeper!

Strategy Focus: Informational text research and written response; comparing text for further details

Materials: Cover, page 166; student directions, page 167; student response sheet, page 168 (two or more per student); trade books related to a current content theme (if you are having your students work on one topic)

Preparing the Station:

1. Glue the cover from page 166 to the front of a large manila envelope. Glue the student directions from page 167 to the back of the manila envelope. Laminate for durability.

2. Put the student record sheets inside the envelope.

3. Put the content trade books that students will use in a basket and display at this station.

Activity Introduction:

1. Show students the model of the response sheet. Explain the student station directions and clarify any questions.

2. Show them resources that are available, but tell them they may use any other books that allow them to find further information about their topic.

3. TIP: You may have all of your students reading books on one particular topic if you are working on a thematic unit of study. This is why we suggest gathering a basket of possible books. If you want them to read independent books and search for other books that go along with that topic, be sure to include some mini-lessons on how to search for books by topic in your media station or classroom library.

Differentiation for All Students:

1. Readers that need additional support may find one alternate book initially to find additional material to extend their learning.

2. Advanced-level readers could choose to develop their extended finding into a new product, such as a poster or brochure, of information on the topic. Adding illustrations with captions would be a great way to incorporate visual literacy into this activity as well.

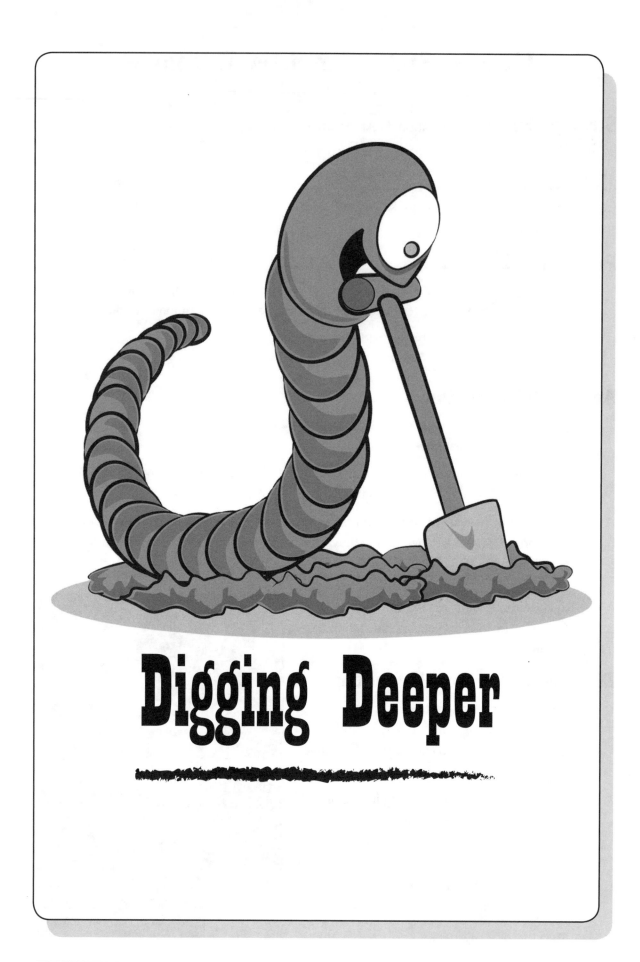

Digging Deeper

Digging Deeper

Directions:

1. Find two non-fiction books that are about the same topic as a non-fiction book that you are currently reading.

2. Take a Digging Deeper Response Sheet from the envelope.

3. Write your name, date, and title of your current book on the top of the response sheet. Record the topic that you are investigating.

4. Write a summary of important information you learned from this book in the summary box.

5. Next, use two other books about the same topic. Read in each one to find further information about this topic. Can you find additional details about what you already learned?

6. In each New Text Box, record the title of the new book you found, and write any information you learned that helped your thinking go even deeper about this topic. Great digging! (Keep your paper in your Station Work Folder when you are finished.)

Digging Deeper
Response Sheet

Name _____ Date _____

Current Book Title: _____

Topic: _____

Summary of my first book:
_____
_____
_____
_____
_____
_____
_____

New Text #1:
Title: _____
New information I found while digging deeper:
_____
_____
_____
_____
_____

New Text #2:
Title: _____
New information I found while digging deeper:
_____
_____
_____
_____
_____

Literacy Station: Written Response
Activity: My Reading Journal

Strategy Focus: Write in various formats; Respond to specific questions based on fiction or non-fiction text

Materials: Copied pages 170-176; one two-pocket folder per student and one for station sample; one 9"x 12" brown envelope; one storage basket; 4"x 6" index cards; one metal or plastic book ring

Preparing the Station:

1. Glue student directions on page 170 to the front of the brown envelope. Laminate before use in the station.

2. Put a class set of journal cover pages inside this sample folder for student use.

3. For the student journal sample, glue one copy of the journal cover, page 171, to the front of one two-pocket folder. We suggest laminating the folder for durability.

4. Copy and put a class set of student journal forms, page 172, in the brown envelope.

5. Create your set of journal question cards by cutting out the sixteen cards found on pages 173-176 and individually gluing each to an index card. Hole punch the top left-hand corner and thread together with a book ring. Keep the ring of cards in the brown envelope along with the blank student journal forms.

Activity Introduction:

1. Hold a class discussion to compare writing and reading journals. Many classes are familiar with writing journals, responding to a specific prompt, or free-choice writing. Explain to the students that in this station, they will be creating another type of written journal, but this time they will be answering questions about their anchor text. By choosing their own question, it frees them from some of the constraints they sometimes feel with prescribed, whole-class prompts. We like to tell them that a reading journal is a place to write their thoughts about their reading.

2. Explain the station directions to the students. Clarify and model all steps.

3. Carefully model the steps in making the initial journals.

4. Review how to answer a question fully in a complete sentence. Many students have great difficulty answering all parts of questions and in complete sentences. This station will provide them with repeated opportunities to reinforce this skill.

Differentiation for All Students:

Students who need extra support may work with a buddy or you can have them do peer editing to check one another's completed work before placing it in their journals.

My Reading Journal

1. Take one new journal page from this envelope.

2. Write the date and the title of your book at the top of the page.

3. Choose a question from the ring of questions.

4. Write the question number on your form.

5. Answer your question. Use complete sentences.

6. Check your spelling and punctuation.

7. Put your complete journal page in your journal folder.

My Reading Journal

Name:_____

I started the journal on: _____

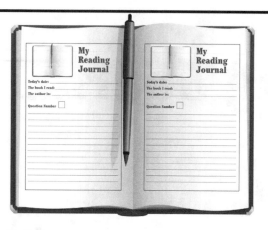

My Reading Journal

Today's date: _____

The book I read: _____

The author is: _____

Question Number ☐

_____

_____

_____

_____

_____

_____

_____

_____

_____

_____

_____

_____

What was your favorite thing about this book?

What did you think about the setting of the book?

Which character did you like best?

What did you learn by reading this book?

Have you read any other books by the same author? What did you notice?

Would you tell a friend to read this book? Why or why not?

What did you wonder when you read this book?

What were your two favorite quotes?

Did you like the way your book ended?

Do you think the photos fit the text? What did you learn from them?

How did the tables or captions help you in the book?

What would you ask the author if you could meet him or her?

What was the problem and solution in the book?

Would you read this book again? Why or why not?

Why did you decide to read this book?

Was there something you disagreed with in your book? Tell about it.

Literacy Station: Written Response
Activity: Nose for News

Strategy Focus: News article writing; Responding to specific headlines and topic questions

Materials: Copied pages 178-180; sample newspaper articles; construction paper; 3"x 5" index cards; one 9 x 12 brown envelope; notebook paper; pencils

Preparing the Station:

1. Glue the student directions, page 178, to the front of the brown envelope. Laminate for durability.

2. Glue actual news articles onto construction paper. Laminate these and display in the station to serve as work samples for the students.

3. Cut topics apart from page 179, and glue individually to the index cards. Laminate, cut, and store in a zip-top baggie in the brown envelope.

4. Make enough copies of the student response sheet (page 180) for your class. Keep in the brown envelope for easy access at the station.

Activity Introduction:

1. Spend time in whole group lessons reading newspaper articles with students and discussing how the who, what, where, when, why, and how questions are answered in news articles.

2. This station is meant to further develop this skill in your students, providing opportunities for deeper thinking about informational text.

3. Explain the student station directions, modeling the steps and clarifying any questions that arise.

Differentiation for All Students:

1. If your students are having difficulty with this activity, you may want to read some articles and find the answers to each question together. Students may enjoy using a highlighter as they find them.

2. For a fun challenge, students can work together to put their individual articles together to create their own unique newspaper. They need to be sure to include headlines and a newspaper title.

Nose for News

Directions:

1. Read several of the newspaper articles that are in the station. This will help you become more familiar with how newspaper articles are written.

2. Select one topic card from the baggie of laminated cards. This will be what you will be writing a newspaper article about.

3. Use one of the student response sheets to create your article. First, plan out the important parts by writing down the answers to the who, what, where, when, why, and how questions of your article. Remember: It has to be about the topic you selected.

4. Now write the article in the space provided. You can continue on the back if necessary. Have fun being a great news reporter!

5. When you are done, put your paper in your Station Work Folder.

Hurricane hits the area   Prize winner announced

Rare butterfly found   Rival teams play tonight

Missing pet   New school built

Record rainfall   Bank robbed

Man helps citizen   Child calls 911

Huge traffic jam   Scientists make discovery

Girl was very lucky   A very dangerous situation

A great act of kindness   An ancient mystery

Best movie picks   Award winners in town

A special family   Great place to travel to

Nose for News

Student Response Sheet

Directions:

1. Using your selected topic, think of how you would respond to each of these questions. Write a brief response on each line.

   - Who? _____
   - What?_____
   - When? _____
   - Where?_____
   - Why? _____
   - How? _____

2. Now use those answers to write your actual newspaper article about that topic in the space below. Be sure to give it a catchy headline!

Literacy Station: Written Response
Activity: What A Character!

Strategy Focus: Character trait descriptions based on reading; Give support and evidence in writing

Materials: Copied pages 182-183; one file folder; student reading folders; independent reading books; pencils

Preparing the Station:

1. Glue the title page 182 to the outside of the file folder.

2. Glue the student directions, page 183, to the top of the inside left of the file folder. Cut words, page 183, and glue to the lower left and the right sides of the folder. (You can choose to cut them into separate words or leave them in blocks.)

3. For durability, we recommend laminating the folder before use in the station.

Activity Introduction:

1. You need to have had mini-lessons on character traits with your students prior to using this station. Have a review briefly, perhaps giving some statements that show character traits of yourself or several of your students. These examples will help clarify the concept for them.

2. Read and explain the specific station directions to the students. Emphasize how they must find a sentence from their book that supports, or proves, why they selected the six traits they chose.

Differentiation for All Students:

1. For students who need additional support, allow them to select fewer than the designated six traits. Working with a partner may help them develop a better understanding of character traits.

2. Challenge more confident readers by having them come up with additional traits not listed. They may want to use a thesaurus to help them with this.

What a Character!

What a Character!

Directions: Find <u>six</u> traits to describe your character. Write a sentence from the book that supports/proves why each one describes that character. Save this paper in your Station Work Folder.

bossy	self-confident
dishonest	practical
unfriendly	open-minded
talkative	trustworthy
sneaky	reliable
rambunctious	motivated
eager	likable
enthusiastic	independent
friendly	humorous
honest	helpful
intelligent	flexible
generous	forgiving
helpful	gentle
inventive	humble
responsible	imaginative
loyal	firm

Resources

Table Talk Guidelines

When you are meeting for a Table Talk Time, please follow these guidelines:

1. Use a "buzz" voice. That means only you and your partner should be able to hear one another.

2. Complete the first step of the Table Talk Log independently. Remember to include the title, author, and genre of your anchor text.

3. Find your Table Talk partner and discuss the facts or events you wrote about. When you are listening to each other speak, be a polite listener.

4. Ask your partner some questions about his or her book.

5. Complete the reflection and sign each other's Table Talk Log. Put your paper in your Station Work Folder.

6. Thank your partner for sharing with you today.

Name:_____ Date:_____

Table Talk Log

Book Title: _____

Author: _____

Genre: _____

1. Your Job:

Write about some of the most interesting events or facts you read in this book:

-

-

-

2. Meet with your Table Talk partner (or group) to share your Table Talk Logs. Ask questions about the books you are sharing.

3. Your Partner's Job:

Your Table Talk partner will write a reflection in the space below about what he or she heard you say. Sign each other's paper and put this paper in your Station Work Folder.

Reflection: _____

_____

_____

_____

Signature of Table Talk Partner: _____

No interruptions please!

Is this a 3B problem?

Remember to...

Ask
3
before
me!

A Quick-Reference Guide to Literacy Stations

Station Name	Activity Title	Fiction	Informational	Both	Page
Comprehension	Author's Study			✔	50
Comprehension	Let's Take a Trip		✔		54
Comprehension	Search and Summarize			✔	58
Comprehension	Senses Brainstorm	✔			61
Comprehension	True/False Trivia		✔		65
Fluency	Found Poem		✔		70
Fluency	Little Buddy			✔	74
Fluency	One-Minute Read			✔	79
Fluency	Reader's Theater			✔	83
Fluency	Recording Studio			✔	87
Listening and Speaking	Computer Presentation			✔	92
Listening and Speaking	Karaoke			✔	96
Listening and Speaking	Merry-Go-Round Reading			✔	99
Listening and Speaking	Question Me			✔	101
Listening and Speaking	Research and Present It		✔		113
Visual Literacy	Create a Model		✔		122
Visual Literacy	Create a Scene	✔			126
Visual Literacy	Food for Thought		✔		131
Visual Literacy	Vocabulary Chains			✔	134
Visual Literacy	Vocabulary Word Art			✔	138
Word Work	Grab a Word, Make a Sentence			✔	142
Word Work	Making Words			✔	144
Word Work	Poetry Place			✔	146
Word Work	Prefix/Suffix Word Play			✔	150
Word Work	Word Gathering			✔	156
Written Response	Create-a-Story Matrix	✔			160
Written Response	Digging Deeper		✔		165
Written Response	My Reading Journal			✔	169
Written Response	Nose for News			✔	177
Written Response	What a Character!	✔			181

Bibliography

Allington, R. L. (2001). *What Really Matters for Struggling Readers: Designing Research-based Programs.* New York: Longman.

Armbruster, Bonnie, Fran Lehr, and Jean Osborn (2001). *Put Reading First: The Research Building Blocks for Teaching Children to Read.* Washington, D.C.: National Institute for Literacy.

Beck, Isabell L., Margaret G. McKeown, and Linda Kucan (2002). *Bringing Words to Life: Robust Vocabulary Instruction.* New York: Guilford Press.

Beers, Kyleen (2003). *When Kids Can't Read, What Teachers Can Do: a guide for Teachers 6-12.* Portsmouth, NH: Heineman.

Daniels, Harvey (2002). *Literature Circles: Voice and Choice in Book Clubs and Reading Groups.* 2nd ed. Portland, ME: Stenhouse.

Dudley-Marling, Curt and Patricia Paugh (2004). *A Classroom Teacher's Guide to Struggling Readers.* Portsmouth, NH: Heinemann.

Fielding, Linda, and P. David Pearson (1994). "Reading Comprehension: What Works?" *Educational Leadership* 51, 5:62-67.

Fountas, Irene, and Gay Su Pinnell (2001). *Guiding Readers and Writers, Grades 3–6.* Portsmouth, NH: Heinemann.

_____. (2006). *Teaching for Comprehending and Fluency: Thinking, Talking and Writing About Reading, K-8.* Portsmouth, NH: Heinemann.

Harvey, S., and Goudvis, A. (2000). *Strategies That Work: Teaching Comprehension to Enhance Understanding.* Portland, ME: Stenhouse.

Keene, E. O., and S. Zimmerman (1997). *Mosaic of Thought.* Portsmouth, NH: Heinemann.

McGregor, Tanny (2007). *Comprehension Connections: Bridges to Strategic Reading.* Portsmouth, NH: Heinemann.

Mooney , Margaret E. (1990). *Reading to, with, and by Children.* Katonah, NY: Richard C. Owen.

Nagy, W. (2003). *Teaching Vocabulary to Improve Reading Comprehension.* Urbana, IL: National Council of Teachers of English.

Nations, Susan, and M. Alonso (2006). *More Primary Literacy Centers.* Gainesville, FL: Maupin House.

Pearson, P. David, and M. Gallagher (1983). "The Instruction of Reading Comprehension," *Contemporary Educational Psychology* 8.

Rasinski, T. (2004). *Assessing Reading Fluency*. Honolulu: Pacific Resources for Education and Learning, available at http://www.prel.org/products/re_/assessing-fluency.pdf.

_____. (2003). *The Fluent Reader: Oral Reading Strategies for Building Word Recognition, Fluency, and Comprehension*. New York: Scholastic Professional Books.

Routman, Regie (2000). *Conversations: Strategies for Teaching, Learning, and Evaluating*. Portsmouth, NH: Heinemann.

_____. (2003). *Reading Essentials: The Specifics You Need to Teach Reading Well*. Portsmouth, NH: Heinemann.

_____. (2008). *Teaching Essentials: Expecting the Most and Getting the Best from Every Learner, K-8*. Portsmouth, NH: Heinemann.

Serafini, Frank, and S. Serafini-Youngs (2006. *Around the Reading Workshop in 180 Days: a month-by-month guide to effective instruction*. Portsmouth, NH: Heinemann.

Tomlinson, C. A. (2001). *How to Differentiate Instruction in Mixed-Ability Classrooms* (2nd ed.). Alexandria, VA: Association for Supervision and Curriculum Development.

_____. (1999). *The Differentiated Classroom: Responding to the Needs of All Learners*. Alexandria, VA: Association for Supervision and Curriculum Development.

Wolf, M., and T. Katzir-Cohen (2001). *Reading Fluency and its Intervention. Scientific Studies of Reading*. (*Special Issue on Fluency*, edited by E. Kameenui and D. Simmons.) 5: 211–238.

Index